Hope you enjoy
the journey!

Josefa Paul

Finding Patterns

TRAVELING FOUR WOMEN'S PATHS

JOSEFA PACE, PH.D.

Copyright © 2016 Josefa Pace, Ph.D.

All rights reserved. No part of this book may be used or reproduced by any means, graphic, electronic, or mechanical, including photocopying, recording, taping or by any information storage retrieval system without the written permission of the author except in the case of brief quotations embodied in critical articles and reviews.

Archway Publishing books may be ordered through booksellers or by contacting:

Archway Publishing
1663 Liberty Drive
Bloomington, IN 47403
www.archwaypublishing.com
1 (888) 242-5904

Because of the dynamic nature of the Internet, any web addresses or links contained in this book may have changed since publication and may no longer be valid. The views expressed in this work are solely those of the author and do not necessarily reflect the views of the publisher, and the publisher hereby disclaims any responsibility for them.

Any people depicted in stock imagery provided by Thinkstock are models, and such images are being used for illustrative purposes only.
Certain stock imagery © Thinkstock.

ISBN: 978-1-4808-3544-3 (sc)
ISBN: 978-1-4808-3545-0 (e)

Library of Congress Control Number: 2016912401

Print information available on the last page.

Archway Publishing rev. date: 11/17/2016

CONTENTS

Acknowledgements vii
Introduction ix

PART I MEETING THE FOUR WOMEN

Chapter 1   Childhood in Occupied Italy 1
Chapter 2   Naturalization, Welcome to East New York 12

PART II SETTING UP RESIDENCES

Chapter 3   Matilde's Spirit 35
Chapter 4   Susan "Namaste" 49
Chapter 5   Pasqualina's Garden, Whole Food 66
Chapter 6   Filomena's Preserve and the Culture of Airola 82
Chapter 7   "Speak Airola" through Tradition 91

PART III WEIGHTED LABELS

Chapter 8   The Weight of the Dead 105
Chapter 9   The Storm 112

Epilogue 121
Recipes 123
Idiomatic Expressions from Airola 153
Endnotes 155
About the Author 159

*Italicized words in the text are direct quotes spoken by the women.

ACKNOWLEDGEMENTS

I would like to give a loving hug ("dare un abbraccio d'amore") to the four women--Pasqualina, Susan, Matilde, Filomena, and their families who are more than a source of inspiration. I find tremendous strength in their will to change and shift mindsets--including my own. I am extremely grateful to witness the trustworthiness of deep-rooted friendships. The women each created a space that was hospitable and sustainable, and the women exude a social and mental ethos which is lacking within 21st century collective communities.

I began to know these women, through their oral storytelling. *Finding Patterns: Traveling Four Women's Paths* could not be possible without the help of all the family members who took the time to sit and speak with me "at the table." Thank you to my generous parents, especially my mother for creating the heritage recipe section. Special gratitude for the relentless support shown by my sister, brother, and brother and sister-in-law. Also, thank you, Sasha, for reading through the narrative and offering comments, and my dear friends for their constant encouragement throughout the process.

Finding Patterns: Traveling Four Women's Paths is dedicated to Pasqualina who "took care of me" in many ways. She let me use her house and garden for play. She transformed the functions of pots and pans into exciting beats of amusement.

INTRODUCTION

Learn your trade and put it on the side
--Imparati l'arte e mettelo al' parte

What is the secret to reaching 80 years of age and living past this number?

We live in a world that changes at exponential rates. We live through uncontrolled warfare and terror attacks, frequent catastrophic events, and rapid technological advances. Because of this instability, the term "permanent home" is not relative.

The four women:
- lived through constant bombing during WII in an occupied Italy
- lived during the reign of dictators
- survived immigration to New York and became citizens
- migrated and set up permanent residences globally
- provided financial support for their families
- worked as seamstresses within factories ("sweat shops") and were part of unions
- witnessed transitions in American, Argentinian, and Italian cultures and politics
- and now, live among the millennials in the digital age

They are adaptable and trans-lingual and have little formal education. Yet, they are model life coaches for our generation. Trends in the 21st century have highlighted naturally grown vegetation and cooking practices. Mental health and fitness present strong and healthy images of beauty. Finding time for mindfulness is combated by constant violent threats, economic uncertainty, and environmental disaster.

When I look at these women, I ask: "How have they functioned on a day-to-day basis for over 80 years with such drastic and rapid shifts socially, physically, mentally, economically, environmentally and technologically? What are their perceptions? How do they cope?"

Lady Gaga and Tony Bennett "Cheek to Cheek" Live! On PBS

My academic advisor suggested that I view Lady Gaga and Tony Bennett's performance "Cheek to Cheek" and focus upon the song, "Ev'ry Time We Say Goodbye." Lady Gaga began introducing the song by expressing, "This is for my grandmas." She continued, "This one is for my grandmas. They are both here tonight, Ronnie and Ang. Two Italian ladies make me very strong. They have been through so much both of em...and...because they went through so much they taught me so much. And it was all that wisdom, I know that's why I am here today. So thank you. This is for you grandmas" (Lady Gaga, 2015).

The four Italian women--Pasqualina Ruggiero, Matilde Mauro, Assunta Rufrano, and Filomena Lamberti--were born between 1928-1936 in Southern Italy, and immigrated to the United States after World War II. These women lived within their means and acquired a set of resources that carried them throughout their trails. They read situations, coped, and fled their native land at a point in time. These decisions were all made with little formal education. These women are deeply rooted within their communities. They carry with them mental weight, and while lacking in physical mobility at over eighty years of age, their essence vibrantly spreads to the family. They are master chefs, wine connoisseurs, and spiritual advisors. They are constantly sustaining other people's lives, and, so now we celebrate them and learn from their ways, remember their contributions, especially during a time in history where we need desperately to hold onto their empathetic ethos.

The importance of knowing these four women is that each of them is currently in her mid-80s. If they do not orally tell the private history of their lives, then their stories, cultures, and languages are lost. These are personal narratives which are a part of a public history. There are many parallels in their words, and they can influence young people in the present because of their experiential skills. Coming to understand their unique personalities and intentions allow for others to learn from these talented unconventional women and demonstrates longstanding techniques of wit and survival that weathers storms and conflicts.

Finding Patterns: Traveling Four Women's Paths is a story about extra-ordinary people. They are not deemed politicians, leaders, diplomats or elitists. However, they are the true grassroots' agents who are images of hope and change. Their stories can appeal to so many. The immigrant experience is explicitly reflected as so many currently, have migrated across countries and continents and are separated from their families as they undergo a naturalization process for a "better life." Cheer for the working class underdogs!

Women of all ages, grandmothers, mothers, and daughters understand the imbalances of life. We live during a tumultuous era and look for role models. Several students and friends share stories, and they battle with significant issues. These women are markers of strength and courage so we do not despair and withdraw to the dark places in our minds as we cope with heartache, grief, loss, sadness, doubt, unemployment, debt, and relational mysteries of our time. The four women are also the socialites of all celebrations. They capitalize on any moment to 'party' and gather for dance, cheer, food, and drink.

It is difficult to build internal strength, and it is becoming more challenging to find this quality among men and women consistently. The four women raise the bar in all areas of life. They have undergone much tragedy, and yet, are mentally tough. They remain self-sufficient and go beyond the label of "domestic." Each loves a side or the different sides to being an Italian. This nonfiction narrative cradles the women's words and gives them agency. It is hard not to respect their trials and grow to care about their life's journey; and allow their lives to influence our own behaviors and attempt to connect to some of their moral fibers.

Finding Patterns: Traveling Four Women's Paths is comprised of three parts. In Part I, we are introduced to the women who are living in an occupied Southern Italy during WWII. They are between the ages of nine and fourteen. Immediately after, two of the four women make their way to New York by boat, and sometime after the war, the other two women immigrate to New York also. In Part II, each of the women assemble homes that have a multi-level purpose. Walking tours of their houses along with daily tasks that consume their days are presented. The narrative illustrates the nonlinear travels of the four women through spaces like Monte Grande, Argentina; Surprise, Arizona; Wantagh, New York; and Airola, Italy. The final chapter in the section commemorates the origins and customs of Airola, Italy over time. Part III includes chapters that display how the women impact one another's lives and the lives of their families in the present. Events that are described in this section are a funeral, the aftermath of Hurricane Sandy, and the pre-storm happenings. As the four women come to the final chapter in their lives, their significant others are gradually passing on and they are trying to hold steadfast. Their bodies are dwindling and so is what they can manage. Slowly, their gardens are cut down each year, but their belief in family is the cement that holds. *Finding Patterns: Traveling Four Women's Paths* also provides idiomatic expressions that the women learned while growing up in Airola. These expressions begin each chapter and more phrases are included at the end of the text. Many Southern Italian recipes are also shared at the back of the book so that others can participate in the joys of feast.

Those who are brought up to value the Italian culture, literature, language, and food can relate to the mindsets and traditions of the Italian origins. Most studying Italian culture have read the epic classic, Dante's *Divine Comedy*, where he is narrating the images of the afterlife--hell, purgatory, and heaven through poetics. Pasqualina is the immediate source in beginning the oral retelling and introducing us to her friends. Each of their childhoods starts in the "hell" of war. Their time in New York places them on a path of limbo and indecision, and their next road in life is depicted in their final resting place. Along this journey is an assisted presence, Phyllis, Pasqualina's daughter. Phyllis is like a Virgil--a guide, inquisitor, navigator--to these women who she knew in a more remote past. Phyllis speaks the women's language fluidly. The book compiles the oral stories, emails, letters, shared Facebook images, interviews with the women, and conversations with family members to create a written document of the four women's lives.

BRIEF INTRODUCTION TO THE KEEPER OF THE STORIES

I am wholesale, says Pasqualina Ruggiero.

At eighty-two, Pasqualina steps slowly with a sturdy walking cane, her *new friend*. She places the cane against the kitchen wall and sits herself at the table, a familiar place for her. The kneading board is in front of her. She asks for a smooth bottomed glass and a ruler. *Watch me*, she tells the two other generations who are around her. She begins to cut and measure pieces of baking dough so each piece is the same size. *48 Tea tarts*. Rhythmically, authentically, and with gusto she rolls the dough and divides the pieces, flattens it with the bottom of the round glass, and places the dough into the individualized small muffin pan. She has been making dough since she was six years old. Pasqualina was a seamstress for most of her life in America, but she is the matriarch for her children and grandchildren all of her life. When she was sewing in the factory, located in the East New York section of Brooklyn, she understood that her job was to build patterns from *scratch*. If she did not sew the stich correctly, she had to figure it out or sometimes rip out the stitches. She considered herself *wholesale* because she was creating the pattern not the design of the dress.

Grandmothers tell stories over the course of their lives. They recite the stories often to their families. But these four Italian immigrant women, in particular, teach life lessons at the kitchen table where they cook and eat with the family. Pasqualina Ruggiero turned eighty years old when I began to formally write her story. She was a granddaughter and daughter and is a mother and grandmother. Her grandchildren spent time at her house before and after school. Whether she came to their houses or they were brought to her house before the start of the school day, she had a glass of orange juice and daily vitamins waiting. After school at her house, she had a hot snack. It was beans with manest or (verdura) or a pasta dish. Afterwards, they ate her homemade anisette cookies. She watched her grandchildren play in her backyard. The garden was full of life and love. The garden had a cement area connecting it to the garage. Every August, on this cement area, homemade sauce and wine were produced. She developed her grandchildren's imaginations as they would either kick a ball against the garage brick wall, have a pass with their grandfather, or make up a dance using the grass or the living room area as a dance floor. The garage window broke three times and so did the living room glass table. The kids would hide under the covers in her bedroom in fear that she would yell. Pasqualina would not yell, but told her grandchildren to rest.

She told her grandchildren her life stories and about her friends through intimate conversations. She encouraged them to write and call her friends. She was the source and intermediary for documenting the oral stories of the past and linking the connections with Susan, Matilde, and Filomena. It was through Pasqualina's conversations that we are introduced to people in her life. It was through digital and auditory advances in technology which enabled the initial contact with the other women. It is through these beautiful women that we continue to grow in our relationships, perceptions, understandings, and have the ability to create ties.

Part I

MEETING THE FOUR WOMEN

CHAPTER ONE

Childhood in Occupied Italy

One time you're born and one time you're dead
--Una volta si nasce e una volta si muore

Once the war finished, we were scared and lived on fear, said Pasqualina in 2010. She sat at her kitchen table sipping her demitasse coffee. At almost eighty, Pasqualina was known to refer to the war quite frequently throughout her life. Each time she spoke of the war, it was in fragments. The repeated image retold was of the bombs falling from the sky. History books discuss modern warfare during World War II. Pasqualina expressed the grave danger that clouded her childhood. Bombs fell one by one and at multiple times. Her eyes and gestures revealed the visual in her mind. She did not describe the sound but made the noise. She closed her eyes and mimicked the vibrations. She spoke of this ingrained memory through the movement of her head and hands.

Her life was more than interrupted. It revolved around survival tactics. She and her family ate what they could find because the Germans stole their pigs. This memory was vivid. Her mother kept large pigs that were 300 pounds. When the Germans had taken them, they cut the pigs' heads off in front of her. It started with their source of food being severed. Then, they had to hide Pasqualina's older brother, Nicola, in the fields, farmhouse, or with her grandparents who lived closer to the mountains so that the Germans would not recruit him to fight. She faced the possibility of losing her brother if she made an error when communicating with the enemy. The German army blew up a walking bridge that was close to their home, and so, Pasqualina's family could not escape into the next town. By crossing the bridge, this would give them a passageway into the mountains and away from danger. The bridge was not restored until the Americans came.

During this time, she and her family could not reach the market place. It was on Thursdays that meat could only be given out as rations, and it was never enough. This phase of her life she categorized as *hell*. At ten years old she went through the 'hell of war' and has carried the fears, images, and feelings for over seventy years. She could not imagine being without these prompted trepidations; and no one explained to her the possibility of imagining anything differently. *We didn't have dreams.*

Pasqualina Lamberti's parents, Grazia and Donato were married in 1926. She was born on October 27, 1932 in Airola, Benevento, Italy. Her father's parents and siblings *went back and forth* to the United States and Italy during the early part of the 20th century. Donato was born in the United States. He married Grazia in Italy. During WWII, he was already working in the United States, and then was *called* to serve in the U.S. army. After the war, he worked sanitation in New York. Pasqualina's father was not around for the first eight years of her life. He did not know his own daughter. He could not come back to Italy during World War II because he was not allowed. He wrote to his wife through letters, and she needed someone to read the letters to her. Pasqualina's mother did not attend school. She signed her *name with a cross* (meaning an x).

When Pasqualina was born, her mother named her, Pasqualina. In one of the letters Pasqualina's father expressed that he wanted his daughter's name to be Anna. Her mother went to city hall in Italy to change the name. For the first ten years of her life, Pasqualina would be called Anna. It was not until the war ended and she came to the United States that they realized her name was not legally changed. In the United States, she officially was known as Pasqualina while her family still called her Anna.

Pasqualina began attending school in Airola when she was five. It was 1937 and her primary school was not in one location. Rooms were setup to be on multiple streets. For the next five years she learned to sew from dress makers. She also learned science, math, reading, and writing the alphabet. They spoke the Italian (dialect) from the town. Her understanding was that you completed up to the fifth grade in Italy. It was not typical for anyone in the area to go beyond fifth grade unless you were to become a doctor or teacher. *Nobody did it.* Since her father was not present throughout her childhood years, she and her family had to farm. They cultivated the farm and raised crops. Her brother, Nicola, and sister, Lucia, raised potatoes, wheat, corn, and all kinds of vegetables. They would not allow her to farm because she was too frail. Her family thought she was sick since she could not gain weight, and they did not want her to perform laborious tasks in the field. Her family raised wheat. They helped cut and bundle it. A machine would plow the fields, and young girls would place the tied bundles over their heads and carry them. When Pasqualina recalled this act, she thought of Sophia Lauren in the film *Monte Cassino*. Every Sunday Pasqualina's family went to visit her grandparent's house in the mountains and had a meal.

Since Pasqualina's family were farmers, she was well aware of the separation between the city people and her life. Her younger days were spent going to school and coming home to cook and clean-- typical, domestic chores. With the war, the divide in socioeconomic status did not exist. People from the city would come into her town to hide. Pasqualina felt she lived better in her community because they appreciated the land, but people from the outside looked at her and her family as uneducated.

Assunta Melisi was Pasqualina's childhood friend who lived and went to school in Airola.[1] Assunta recalled Pasqualina leaving school a few years before she did. At this time, Assunta (shortened to Susan) was about fourteen years old and was on the middle school level. The two young girls were separated when Susan had the opportunity to attend school in the city. As they began different life paths, they did not see each other much—but when speaking to Susan at the age of seventy-nine, she made it clear, that she was still *Anna's good friend*. Susan's father also tried to create a home in New York during the depression years. She had no contact with her father for three years. Her father *ended up somewhere on some farm* in the U.S. for room and board and was with Pasqualina's father who was *trying to make ends meet doing the same kind of work*.

While visiting and interviewing Susan in Surprise, Arizona, in 2010, Susan was seated at the kitchen table and embraced the camera as it recorded her voice. Assunta Melisi was born in 1932 in Airola, Benevento, Italy. She received the nickname Susan when she came to New York. She was named Assunta because she was born on the Feast of the Assumption, August 15th. When she was three or four years old, she was sick and a variety of doctors were treating her for *different things*, and they never found anything. Her grandfather searched for a doctor and took her to Naples, and the doctor said, "You waited until this child was half dead before you brought her here." Susan had intestinal problems, pneumonia, and was being treated for other things. She was weak. The doctor told her grandfather, "We can save this child if we do everything exactly as I say." Her grandfather responded, "Do whatever it takes even if I have to sell my farm."

Giuseppe and Francesca Barisciano were Susan's parents. Susan lived with her grandfather and mother in Airola. Her grandfather was the head of the household because her father was in the States. Her grandmother died when she was three years old. After she died her paternal grandparent lived in this huge house. He relished in the accomplishments of his farm life. He took Susan through his garden and began to tell her of new plants growing. He told her it was going to have *cachi*--persimmons. They had a chestnut tree. He explained that it was *prickly, like a porcupine* and would fall to the ground when ripe. *He was quite a sportsman*. Her grandfather would like to hunt and shoot little quails with the bee bee gun, and he would be excited to eat the quail the next day.

Unlike Pasqualina's mother, Susan's grandparents were able to read and write *because they were raised by these rich people*. Her grandfather was fluent in reading in Italian. He was able to communicate so well in that he did not have to farm himself. He had people working for him. She remembered as a girl *all these guys would come to the house to get paid*, and he would pay them and give them coffee. He was well read and *he subscribed to agricultural places because it was very intriguing to him to raise crops that were unusual. Fruit we have here* (meaning Arizona), *I have eaten it in Italy from our own place because he was able to graft it just for the hell of it. He was able to do it. My grandfather was quite the dapper guy.*

Her father did not directly write to her, but he would write one letter to her mother and a little note for the kids. *In fact, when it was WWII and I was in Italy I remember dad had always stressed to my mom to have an education…to keep me in school. That's why Anna and I got separated. I went to what was then called a preparation school and I had to stay in Benevento for two to three weeks for preparation.* Susan experienced the bombing in Benevento. It became unsafe, and she left for her town, so she did not complete her schooling.

At thirteen, Susan's life became a stand still where fear became an everyday encounter. She went back to her home farming town. *We were getting invaded by the Germans and the Germans began to take over.* She expressed a sincere nostalgia when she spoke of the Germans taking *our* land. She recalled the extreme sadness her grandfather felt as they trampled over the dirt, the garden, and his pride. His agricultural show was destroyed, and he was devastated. *It became worse because when the Germans were losing and the Americans were coming in they were doing a lot of spite work. They were raiding everybody. I remember digging holes of whatever treasure…and hiding it in there because at that time the gold had to be destroyed.*

When Susan was growing up, they were not given a *vision* for the future. It was simply that they would learn to be homemakers and would receive the little amount of school offered. Like Pasqualina, they learned from people who mastered professional dressmaking—similar to an apprenticeship program. They allocated time for a few hours in dressmaking, and then they would have the students partake in another task of experiential learning. Susan expressed that the nuns treated her well in school. During her childhood years, Susan learned to sew, crochet, and embroider. She often observed from afar and was fascinated at how the people within the city dressed and lived. This intensified her desire to come to America. Her mother told Susan that there was a machine that swept the floor. She wondered *how can a machine sweep the floor?* Her father filled her head with these ideas so that when she finally met him in America, there would be plenty, and it would be luxurious. The reality was that before leaving Italy, Susan's schooling ceased and the Germans took her farmland, her *home*.

Filomena Ruggiero sat at her kitchen table in the native town of Airola, Italy with her husband, Pasqualino, and her daughter, Lucy. Filomena was eighty-four years old at the time, and lives in the house across the road from where Pasqualina recalled the Germans stealing her families' livestock. Filomena recounted the Germans shooting and killing their neighbors and townspeople. She and everyone would run to shelter. This was unlike any clash of clans; it was real life. Bomb after bomb kept falling. Filomena spoke the language of her town. She described the war as horrible--*brutta cosa*. She repeated these words. In her silence, her husband would fill in her unspoken words. He spoke passionately, "It was as if the Germans were shooting for the sake of shooting. Shot after shot." Filomena repeated--the bombs. *The bombs, eh bomba. You could see them passing.* Her cousin went to play with a hand grenade and it exploded. She explained that a way out from the danger was to her grandmother's house. The house

was a good distance away from the farm. Filomena described those who got out as *little chickens* running to safety. They had to run or the Germans were going to kill them. Filomena spoke in circles about the war. Through her limited and circuitous language, she kept returning to how bad the war was for her. The bombs translated as an explosive weapon with a violent release of energy; this idea buzzed in her mind.

Filomena Ruggiero was born in 1928 in Airola, Benevento, Italy. Filomena's father was in America before the war. He worked on the railroad line. In 1946, he returned to Italy and did not want his family to experience the depression of America. Filomena explained that her father would rather die in Italy of hunger than to have his family and children go to the United States and live through the depression in which he lived through in New York. It was understood, too, that if a permanent job was not in place in the States, families were not invited to come. Only if her father could support them in the United States would they have gone. They stayed in Italy during the aftermath of World War II.

Filomena was one of six children. The eldest of the family was her brother, Tomaso. He died while serving in the Italian Navy during the war. She said *he had a good head on his shoulders and was able to join the Italian Navy.* Filomena was the second child. Her younger sister is Vincenza, and her younger brother is Giuseppe (this would later be Pasqualina's husband). The youngest in the family were Antonio and Francesco. They were twins, however, Francesco died at the age of three.

During the war, Filomena understood that Mussolini mandated children to be in school. He wanted them to learn how to read and write. They were required to learn and attend at least up to the fifth grade so they would be *able to sign their name instead of making a cross for their written signature.* She believed that he wanted young Italian children to be little soldiers and wear a uniform.

Before she went to school, she had to gather string beans from the garden and cook them. When in school, she did learn to read and write. She did not find reading pleasurable. She was interested in history and geography. She was fascinated by geography. Filomena wanted to know everything about world matters. History informed her about geography, and she learned about World War I.

Finding Patterns

In 2010 in Montegrande, Argentina, Matilde Mauro began to speak in her Argentinian tongue about World War II. Her daughter, Lucy, translated her words. *Everyone left the area and went to the trees. They would make tunnels and then cover it with fallen trees and branches. If confronted by enemy soldiers, a gun was pointed in your face so that you would tell the truth. It was probably to scare you if you were hiding a soldier.* Her grandmother used to put something inside her grandfather's shoes so that it would raise his fever higher, and when the Germans came, they would not take him because he was ill. In the same breath she continued, *when the Americans came, the Americans were full of lice. They never changed their clothes. But they did bring sliced bread with marmalade.* It was the first time she had seen marmalade on slices of bread.

The area in Italy in which Matilde lived was primitive; though most southern roads would be considered underdeveloped. There were dirt roads and a horse and carriage came through on it. She and her siblings were sent to hide with their grandparents. She had a total of eight siblings. A pair of twins died as infants. When Matilde was twelve years old, her father volunteered to fight in Africa. She would not see him until they reunited in Argentina.

Matilde Tauro was born in 1936 in Roccafinadamo, Penne, in the Province of Pescara. Roccafinadamo is north of Airola and about

195 kilometers east of Rome and about 200 kilometers east of Monte Cassino. Matilde was born to Lucia Melchiorre and Domenico Tauro. Her mother did not read or write, and she stayed home with her children. Her father was able to read and write and took work where it was available. He was mostly a day laborer for farmers. During the war, he volunteered and was sent to Tripoli for a *long time*. After, Matilde's father went to Argentina in 1949.

Matilde vehemently repeated that she did not like going to school in Italy. But, she liked to learn, because she did not want to be *dumb*. She remained in the first grade three times. She played in the school yard and liked to draw. She did attend school up to the sixth grade. Matilde indicated that the school was *seven or eight kilometers away*. People stayed in school until 6 p.m. because they could not travel. After Matilde finished her school day, she went to work construction.

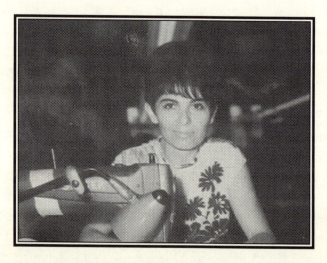

Matilde was nineteen years old when she left Roccafinadamo to go to Buenos Aires. It took six years for her family to arrive in Argentina. She lived in a pre-and postwar Italy. It was from 1936-1955. However, Matilde struggled to connect to her Italian roots. Matilde struggled to connect to her Italian roots. She did not want to go into further detail because she felt Italy *did not give her or her family anything*. What she held onto were the documents of her origin and the tarnished pictures of her past. *In case we need them,* she said. The terse narrative depictions and the documents were the evidence of her existence in Italy.

These documents present a backdrop and a discovery of a static past. Matilde has several documents. She has materials from the British Legion commemorating her father's service in Africa during WWII. It was an actual letter to the prime minister in the UK, possibly a letter written by a lawyer on behalf of her father during WWII. The document was written in Italian.

In 1946 after the war ended, Matilde and Filomena remained in Italy, and Pasqualina and Assunta's fathers finally called their families to come to New York. Pasqualina and Assunta immigrated together on the *Marina Shark* boat from Naples, and it took three weeks for them to journey to America before arriving on Ellis Island. Pasqualina traveled with her mother, Grazia, her brother, Nicola, and sister, Lucia; and Susan came with her mother and younger sister, Clara. In Italy, when Susan pursued further education in the city area, away from the farming town, she and Pasqualina remained friendly, but they were not in frequent contact. The war ended their separation and brought them to America. They lived in the same apartment building in the East New York section of Brooklyn and stayed close friends for over 70 years.

CHAPTER TWO

Naturalization, Welcome to East New York

Who goes slow goes far
--Chi va piano va lontano

Pasqualina immigrated to the United States in 1946 and was enrolled in a public middle school. She continued onto a vocational high school. Her mother commuted to New York City for work. She took the subway and would count the stops because she could not read the signs. Despite Pasqualina's parents being unable to read or write, her parents were adamant about her attending school. Pasqualina felt that since her parents could not speak English because they were not fluent in their own native language, that her mother knew the importance of education. English was a struggle for her father to learn despite working in the United States for several years before the family immigrated.

Pasqualina continued her education at thirteen years old in East New York and went to a junior high school. It was a trade school for high school students. She was the only person in her family to receive a high school diploma. Her sister merely went to school for two years and then she worked in the factory with their mother, and their brother worked in construction. Pasqualina's parents worked laborious tasks. Her mother was a seamstress in a factory, and her father worked sanitation in Brooklyn. She lived on Bergen Street, No. 2024. Susan lived in the apartment upstairs from Pasqualina. It was a three-floor apartment building. The area did not reflect the monotonous farm life of Airola, but their families seized this vision of another possibility to survive and thrive. American schooling and work life offered a path that could possibly place more than food on the table, but opened other avenues for working class families.

Pasqualina and Susan once again attended school together. The girls figured out that they would eventually have to learn English. Otherwise, if you did not know the word, the teacher would hit you. Pasqualina *simply read* what they told her to read. Susan's dad spoke to the family in Italian because her mom was having a difficult time communicating. The system after immigrating to New York was to make connections with *your own kind* so you could communicate and find work. The girls' families worked with Italian people so they could speak the language from their homeland. Susan's father made the switch to speak English in the household. Her sister, Clara, caught on immediately. In school, Susan felt inferior and self-conscious. She mispronounced words, and if she spoke, others would know she was *foreign*. Pasqualina and Susan had to jump in and learn quickly without any life preservers.

Pasqualina's father thought his daughter would teach the craft of sewing. He encouraged her to continue schooling. Pasqualina studied her trade in school. She maintained contact with her teacher, Mrs. Scalea, until she died. Mrs. Scalea even bequeathed Pasqualina in her will. She respected Pasqualina's work ethic because she was Italian herself. It was in vocational high school where Pasqualina would learn custom design sewing. The students worked on the sewing machines. She went to school, learned her trade, and went to the movies when she could. She became dear friends with Marie, who also attended the school. Not all the "sewing girls" could stay in school. Pasqualina was fortunate that she did not have to drop out. Marie dropped out and had to work and help out the family. She moved to the Bronx, but they continued to see each other on Sundays and would play records and go dancing. *We all came from Italy and did not know much English.* While her skills, traditions, and language were maintained, Pasqualina would never live in Italy again.

She would not visit Italy until well after she was married. Pasqualina's older brother was now marrying Vincenza (Filomena's sister). Vincenza and Filomena would be Pasqualina's future sisters-in-law because Pasqualina would eventually marry their younger brother, Giuseppe. They married men from their town, Airola. Pasqualina's future husband, Giuseppe, could not live in *this country*, meaning the United States because no one was *rooted here yet*. He was *called* to Santo Domingo. Giuseppe left Italy in 1953, and after his sister's wedding, he went to Santo Domingo for a year with a friend, returned to New York, and then had to return to Santo Domingo until Pasqualina called him. He was a *business man* in Santo Domingo. He sold meat, saint memorabilia, and souvenirs-- anything you could find on the street.

When he came to New York in 1954, Pasqualina, at the age of twenty-one, married him. Pasqualina explained that *if you did not get married by twenty-one you were considered an old maid*. They had a church wedding and a "football party" celebration. Small sandwiches were served. Over 400 people were invited to her house to celebrate. Giuseppe could not read or speak English. She said *he still does not know much. He can read a little in Italian*. In Italy, he skipped school often and *played hookie a lot* in third grade. Since he did not speak English, they did not want to grant him an American citizenship. *It was hard to be an American citizen*. Giuseppe became a construction foreman when working in New York. He contributed to the community by assisting to build the Verrazano Bridge along with many other streets in New York City.

Pasqualina worked tirelessly at Seymour's Coat Factory. She was paid a piece rate. Pasqualina was very fast on the machine. No one could surpass her skills. Sometimes she brought the work home, and after dinner, she continued to sew until 4 a.m. The women in the factory resourcefully made clothing or coats for their children for the holidays. Many from the neighborhood worked at Seymour's Coat Factory, which was located on Pacific Avenue in the East New York section of Brooklyn. It was near Our Lady of Loreto Church. The newly married couple, Pasqualina and Giuseppe, began a family and had three children. Their names are Pasquale, Filomena (Phyllis), and Grace. Before Pasqualina went to the hospital to have her last child, she told her husband to bring the work she completed *to the shop*. Pasqualina and Giuseppe lived first in Brooklyn and then moved to Woodhaven.

At a point in time, each of the four women lived, worked, and celebrated their time in the city of New York. Pasqualina said when in New York, *At that time it was a dream to have a job.* She said that her social life was integral. Susan and her husband, another couple, and Pasqualina and Giuseppe were considered very close. They would come to Pasqualina's house and not leave. Pasqualina would *Throw another mattress on the floor* for Susan and her husband. When someone came from Italy to New York, Pasqualina would have them stay in her house. Matilde and her husband spent time in Pasqualina's home. Susan said, *Pasqualina's house was always busy and social.* The New York energy revived their spirits. This was the skeletal beginnings of laying grounded roots for the women.

SUSAN IN NEW YORK

Susan married Danny Rufrano in 1950. Danny had served in the United States Army during WWII. She met Danny when she was sixteen. She was young. His family owned the apartments where Pasqualina and Susan's families were living. Susan's parents did not approve of Danny at first, and because of their disapproval, Susan explained, *I had to live with my uncle in Vermont and so I did not finish high school.*

Susan was eighteen when she got married, and Pasqualina attended her wedding. Since Susan's parents did not favor her decision to get married, Susan described the mood of the wedding as *funeral like.* Eventually, her parents grew to like him. After getting married, she then moved to Commack, Long Island and lived there for nineteen years. Susan had two children. Their names are Theresa and Randy. Since Susan was married first out of the four women, Pasqualina said she taught her *the ways of the world.*

Unfortunately, it was a short marriage. Susan became a widow in 1964 when Danny died of a massive heart attack. Her husband passed when Susan was in her thirties. Pasqualina said that Susan's husband *was such a nice guy, he really loved her...she went through hell after.* Because Pasqualina would push others to eat her homemade cooking, *He would say to me when he came over... Anna the food is on the table. You don't have to force us to eat.* Pasqualina chuckled at herself when she repeated his words.

When he died, Susan's parents were sad. Susan's tone did not shift when telling the story of her husband's life. She remembered *crying at*

night and being the happy go lucky strong person during the day. Susan presented physical artifacts of their life. She displayed pictures of her deceased husband, Danny, and their wedding photo album. These pictures were stored in a box. The images were in black and white. Susan discussed how her children reacted to her husband's death at such a young age. The ways her children remembered her husband were through some of the activities they partook in, much like the ones Susan partakes in now at her community center in Surprise, Arizona.

In Surprise, Arizona, Susan stored another trunk of photos. In the case were photos of her husband, Danny. Upon looking at his picture, one can noticeably see that he was a strikingly handsome man. In the trunk were documents--their marriage certificate was one document. There were many old photographs of Susan and Danny on their wedding day. Other pictures showed Danny sitting beneath the sign of Okinawa in Japan.

The memory of her husband and the artifacts she presented were candid. Most of the black and white photos were that of her and her husband on their wedding day. She saved the photographs when Danny was in Okinawa completing service for the U.S. during WWII. There was a wedding album containing their signatures and names. She had her husband's junior high school diploma. It was as if her husband's brief existence was memorialized. The box was kept in a safe place. In this sense, it was legitimizing her relationship with her husband at an earlier time.

Her son, Randy, rarely spoke about the loss of his father. Her daughter, Theresa, did. Susan would repeat lines to her children like *remember daddy...* It was difficult in losing a parent so suddenly. *Randy and Danny went bowling together and played cards. Randy was a consistent presence at his father's side. Randy would be right next to his father watching him play cards. He was six or seven years old and interpreting what his dad was playing.* Her husband was a very strong family-oriented man, and very compassionate. He acted with integrity and was soft spoken. Susan described him with endearment. After he died she remembered, how her limits were taxed, and it was after the funeral that she was *totally out of it.* Her sister was making some arrangements, and the priest was over, and she tried to shut everybody out. She said *leave me alone, he's gone, what is this going to prove.* Susan had to regroup after the loss of her husband. She was a young mother and needed to keep her family moving forward. She was familiar with this feeling of loss and atonement. This was a personal battle that isolated her; tragedy struck her again, and it uprooted her.

WIDOW'S WORDS: BEING A SINGLE PARENT

It was the summer after Danny passed. Susan took Theresa to work with her. It was a small café in Commack, Long Island. Susan thought that she would not be able to work the summer because the children were home, but the employers told her to bring her daughter to work. It was a family-run operation. Theresa was a young girl, and she did not want to spend her summer at the family coffee shop. Susan dragged her to work. Theresa was determined not to go into the shop. Susan laid into her and said, *You don't have a choice. You cannot do this to me.* Theresa did not care. She said to her mother that she would rather sit in the car. Finally, the owner's daughter came outside to get Theresa and coaxed her. The owner's daughter told Theresa to shadow her. She followed the owner's daughter for about an hour or two. She asked Theresa to bring water and asked her to help clean off some tables. Theresa was given a little bit of money. Ultimately, it was a coffee shop with booths and contained a huge dining room. It had a private executive dining room where Susan was placed. Theresa worked the counter and surprised everyone. The owner was fascinated with her initiative. She earned tips and was asked if she wanted to help out again. She looked at her pocket full of money, and by the end of the summer, she held more than a pocket full of money.

When Susan saw an IHOP open down the road, she encouraged her daughter to seek employment. After six months, she finally brought Theresa, she applied, and she got the job. The cook was young and took a liking to her. Theresa worked her way through college as a waitress.

Susan realized she could not only waitress to make ends meet. She came from an Italian upbringing where everyone saved. An opportunity had arisen to buy a share into a business. She was working as a purchasing agent at Bogner Broadcast and waitressing part-time. The company manufactured a big transmission plant, and Susan worked her way up the ranks. Her son worked at the company at one point. He was an assistant to an assistant--an accountant for the business. The partners in the establishment were consistently fighting. The person her son spoke to on a regular basis was Lenny. Lenny had the largest share of the business, and there was fifteen percent that someone could purchase. Lenny knew someone in France who was interested in this small share. Susan knew of this potential business transaction. She nosed around and asked her son if Lenny was really buying that share or going to keep it. Susan had sold her house at the time. She wanted her son to ask further. Her son teased her, "Oh yeah right, like they are gonna need your money." Susan persisted in wanting to at least meet the guy. Lenny was Italian. He owned a big horse farm in Westbury. *He and his brother knew nothing about the business, and it didn't matter.* She talked sales and continued with small talk. She made it clear to Lenny that she was not rich and that she was putting everything she had into the business. She requested that her son be a manager. *I want my son to get somewhere.* Lenny gave Susan his word that he would always have a position to work there, and they shook hands. From 1983-1990, Susan managed an Au Bon Pain in New York City.

While Susan did not have business experience, she had life experience and determination to make it. She knew what quality food was. Especially in New York, people were demanding and knew what they wanted. If the customer was unhappy, they would voice it. She could tell when it was a good croissant by the looks of it, and she stayed on top of production by watching *the guys*. Susan had a little bit of wholesale and those were the top hotels.

After Susan left Commack, she lived in NYC on 72nd and Broadway. It was a high-rise building near the Hudson River. She lived with Tony, her boyfriend. *It was expensive.* From 1983-1990, she owned and managed an Au Bon Pain on Third Avenue in NYC. She then lived in Bayside for about eight to ten years. She and Tony parted, and she was in Florida for the next five years and then Bethlehem, Pennsylvania for two years. *They would call me a gypsy because I moved around so much.*

After NYC, she was brought to the Poconos by an investment her son made. He bought a pizza place even though he, himself, did not know how to make pizza. She did not believe in a laissez-faire mentality: *you treat your workers right and your workers will work for you, not true,* she remarked. *Young kids would be working for you. After a while, they would become your friends. They would show up to work. If they were screwing up, they were not going to tell you who did it.* She was stern in her belief that *you have to be there and know how to make the product.*

At close to eighty years of age, when Susan recollected this stage of her life, she was homesick for New York City. It was the city she knew and loved. She was familiar with the accessibility of the subway system. She believed everyone needed a chance, and the opportunity should be embraced. She wanted her children to get ahead and have their roots. While Susan embodied her Italian origins, she did not require herself to follow it every day. She adopted the American lifestyle more and more.

FINDING ROOTS 1964-1986 IN NEW YORK

Filomena Ruggiero lived through the war and post war in Italy. She lived in Airola twenty years after the war. Her town would never be fully restored. When she and her daughters were speaking of the time after the war, her daughter, Lucy, said they grew "Tomatoes and potatoes" as a way to make a living.

Cherry tomatoes. Filomena repeated. In Italian--*Pomodoro*.

Filomena was twenty-one years old when she married Pasqualino Lamberti, Pasqualina's cousin. Pasqualino was an Italian soldier during the war. Filomena and Pasqualino dated for eight years. He was eighteen and she was fourteen. The war was just over when they met. (Pasqualine, he is often referred as). They had three children together, Sandina, Lucia, and Michele. Filomena left Italy and came to New York in the winter of 1964 "after Kennedy died." *Eh non buon* (not good). When they arrived, everyone had a house in Brooklyn. All of the aunts, uncles, and cousins lived near each other. They all lived on the *same block*. Filomena worked as a seamstress in the same factory as Pasqualina. Pasqualine worked in construction with Giuseppe. Everyone received pensions from their years of work in the United States.

When Filomena came to America she lived in a three family house. While the school for the children in Italy was located in a church, Filomena's children in the 1960s had to pick up school life very quickly in America. The children did not like elementary school in Italy with the nuns. Lucy, Filomena's daughter, spent almost ten years in the United States. She became fluent in English and left the U.S. after her wedding in 1973 because her husband's ailing parents still lived in Italy. Acquiring citizenship for her family was difficult. The judge asked Filomena's husband if he was a "bad guy." He told the judge that everybody was a deserter at that time of the war.

Filomena left the United States in 1986 to return to Italy. The reason Filomena returned to Italy was because her husband's parents were sick. Her son, Michele (Michael), continued to reside in New York. Her two daughters, Sandina and Lucia, were already in Airola. Filomena was a farmer (laborer) and domestic worker while living in Italy. She returned to Italy and restored the house left by her in-laws. They lived off the land and continued to farm in Airola. Her life was and is in Italy. She considered Italy her home. *Ha piaceva* (I like it). New York was a holding place. It would also be the final place where her entire family would ever live together again.

Passages from Argentina to New York

After leaving Italy, Matilde Tauro stayed in Argentina from 1955-1961. She married Nicola Mauro in 1957--she was twenty-one years old. Nicola was from Airola, Italy. He was friends with Pasqualina's husband. Matilde had three children, Felix, Anna, and Lucy. From 1961-1968, Matilde lived in New York, and in 1968, she brought her children back to Argentina, but remained living in New York with Nicola. In 1974, Matilde and Nicola both returned to Buenos Aires to live with their family, and remained until 1988.

The first time Matilde came to New York from Argentina, Pasqualina housed Matilde and her husband. Any time anyone needed work who came from the area, Pasqualina brought them to the factory. They would sew garments together, and they were paid piece rate. Giuseppe worked construction with Nicola, Matilde's husband. At that time, you had *to squeeze the blood out of the dollar.*

A phrase Pasqualina would repeat frequently. They considered it a sin to waste anything since they came from knowing the ruins of war.

Much of Matilde's immediate family--her brothers, sisters and parents were in Argentina already. Unlike her husband's family, all of Matilde's sisters began to create a life on the tip of South America. Tragically, at a young age, Matilde lost her younger brother, Vincenzo. He was living in Argentina in October, 1962. Matilde was still in New

York. Her younger sister, Giuliana, was with her brother in Lujan. The town of Lujan is known for its cathedral, museum, and carnival festivities. It now has a museum dedicated to the history of travel in Argentina. Through the path to the carnival, you could oversee the river. Across the way were dangling tree branches and a bridge. This was the place where her brother died. He took a boat ride with another girl in Lujan, and his boat tipped and he drowned. Her sister, Giuliana, cannot bring herself to go to Lujan after this horrific incident. Matilde's brother was twenty-eight years old. Matilde's recollection of her brother was specific. She only had one brother. They escaped World War II together, but he could not escape the tragic fall in the river in Lujan.

From 1964-1985, Matilde's children lived in Argentina during the "Dirty War." Lucy, the third child, explained that she and her siblings were living outside of Buenos Aires. Lucy recalled attending college in Buenos Aires in the 1980s, during Argentina's "Process of National Reorganization." When traveling to university, she was taken off the bus, and her ID card was checked. Although Lucy was chastised by her peers while living in Argentina because she was not a full citizen (because her parents lived in the United States and she lived with her grandparents in Buenos Aires), not being an Argentinian citizen saved her. "Sometimes we live the wars between nations as personal events."[2] These public and private experiences were lasting impressions upon Lucy's memory because she was a product of both the history of Argentina and her mother's decisions.

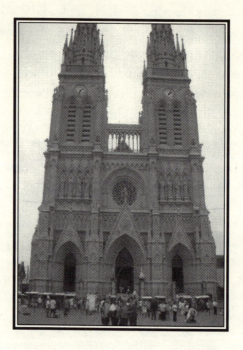

Lucy and her siblings grew up in Monte Grande during the military coups from 1968 to 1983. During this time, the people were not allowed to read much of the writings from Argentinian authors, and the few books they had access to read had to be approved by those in power. Later on, all the writers she read were men, Jorge Luis Borges, Julio Cortazar, Oliverio Girondo, Adolfo Bioy Casares, and some short stories published by Borges and Casares were under a pseudonym, Bustos Domecq. She said that presently in school, more often they would recommend other Latin American writers like Isabel Allende, Gabriela Mistral, Rosa Nissan, and Angeles Mastretta. Lucy was mindful of these narratives.

A common thread among the four women was that they conversed through multiple languages. Questions asked to Matilde were, "What language do you think in? And, what language do you feel most comfortable speaking in?" She did not have an answer. When speaking with Matilde's daughter, the same questions were presented. Lucy responded, "I am equally confused in both."

From 1988-2007, Matilde and her husband returned to New York. The youngest child, Lucy, moved to New York from 1985-2005. Lucy moved back to Argentina in 2005. Matilde and Nicola returned to Argentina in 2007. Matilde fulfilled her dream and became a hairdresser for many years while living in Argentina.

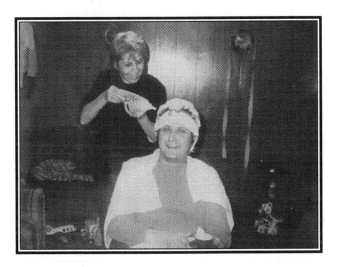

When Matilde, her husband, and Lucy lived in New York, they lived in Queens. Matilde had not been to Somers Street in a long time. When she lived there, she, too, worked in the factory with Pasqualina and her sister in-law, Vincenza. At the Seymour Coat Factory, during working hours, they did not speak at all. A bundle of work was placed in front them, and they went to work on the sewing machine. When you came to New York you did not learn *Ingles* (English) formally. It was acquired. After Matilde came to New York the second time, she worked at Elmhurst Hospital and learned to speak English and

Spanish. There were many Spanish speaking people--*Puerto Rican, Santo Domingo, Venezuelan and Cuban.*

During this time, Lucy, enjoyed the MOMA and the MET and took advantage of what NYC had to offer. She experienced Bastille Day in 2008 in Brooklyn. While there was so much going on in the streets to celebrate the French holiday, there was an Argentinian match on TV and the restaurant-bars on Smith Street were showing the game. Apparently, the area was very popular and "soccer fans were always there. It was a very nice part of Brooklyn. The ambience was pleasant. They had Peruvian food, and you could find everything on the Smith Street strip and watch the U.S. Open."

Lucy was her parents' caretaker. Matilde's husband suffered a stroke in 2001. Lucy helped with the medical paperwork and doctor's visits. Matilde depends on Lucy because she does not drive. Lucy lovingly cared for both of her aging parents. Lucy maintains the communication through email. In 2010, about six months after our visit she wrote. She described the weather seasons in Argentina were opposite than the weather in New York. Her language suggested that it was "another world" and "surreal." She continued to tell us about her mother. She advised her mother to slow down at the age of seventy-seven. As these women age, it was difficult for them to slow down and come to terms with what they may not be able to continue to do. Matilde had a recreational outlet. She spent time with her sister by going to the casinos, which were located about an hour from Monte Grande. Matilde enjoys drinking, smoking, gambling and watching soccer.

While in New York, after Matilde's husband had taken a stroke he was wheelchair ridden. Despite the set-back, they finally settled in Argentina again. Nicola, however, passed in the winter of 2013. Among Matilde's many documents, she secures her marriage certificate that was given to her from the Argentinian Town Hall when she eloped with her Nicola. Matilde carries her citizenship papers from the United States. She still often visits New York to attend to documented paperwork and to see her in-laws. Her stamped American citizenship passport is evidence of her existence across borders. It was through these documents and artifacts that the women were able to "tell stories" of where they had been.

Matilde identified with this hybrid state. She calls herself an American. She does not feel Italian though she appreciated its customs. She received heartache from Italy. New York gave her a chance to restart her life, and she went back to Argentina, the place her family immigrated to after the war. This is where she would remain, with her children, sisters, and grandchildren.

Immigrant Experience in East New York

Typically, during the time between the 1920s-1950s immigrants were encouraged to assimilate into American culture and become patriotic. These women said that when they immigrated to New York, the shifts in language were key to assimilation. They were told to speak English in public spaces and to advance themselves through education. There was an opportunity to upgrade in status. When they came to New York, these women spoke enough English or had people help them use the

language so that they could find a job. Each woman expressed a greater concern for the advancement of their families and wanted to keep the home a safe and social environment. Each of the women spoke Italian in the home. Susan spoke English more in the home than any of the other women. In this way, these women navigated themselves through spaces to succeed in New York, but did not completely assimilate or abandon their linguist roots.[3] They maintained their heritage and cultural beliefs. These Italian or European ideals included both family and community as primary in life and emphasized the importance to remain connected to family locally and abroad. There was an emphasis on sustaining life.

They each mentioned seeing the Statue of Liberty when landing on Ellis Island. New York City was a sign and a place of acceptance for these women. They each expressed gratitude for the financial opportunities and jobs that they worked outside of the home. They created another space for themselves and their families in New York City. New York City is a symbol for peace and hope for those coming from abroad—the ultimate symbol of Lady Liberty.

Part II
SETTING UP RESIDENCES

CHAPTER THREE

Matilde's Spirit

**If you have a basin of gold and you can't wash
your face in it, what good is having it**
--Se ai un bacile di oro e non poui
lavarti la faccia a che serve

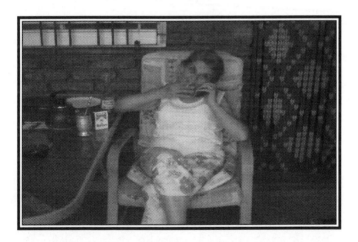

When traveling to Buenos Aires, it can place you in a state of delirium. The travel time can be about fifteen hours when allotting time for connections. Once we landed, the faces we looked for were the familiar ones seen on Skype. Matilde's daughter, Lucy, was hospitable and social. Upon our arrival, Lucy was ready with a carriage to assist with the luggage transport. Driving from the airport to Matilde's house was hazy. After a long trip and being in a half conscious state, the conversation became limited until we finally met Matilde.

When approaching Matilde's home, the car would pause at the entrance until the front gate opened. Then a woman came out whose image was known virtually, through Skype. Matilde embraced us as if we had known her our entire lives. Surrounding Matilde's house in Monte Grande, Argentina was a high-metal gate. In order to enter, a key or log-in was required. Much time was spent in Matilde's backyard because it was summer in January in Argentina.[4] Though her backyard was filled with energy, the heat smothered us. The same energy extended in the home. In the backyard, there was a small in ground-pool, a large barbeque, a bed of grass, plants along the fence line, clothes drying on a rack, and an awning stretching over a patio. In a cage, there was a parrot and it began to speak. The house was made of brick. The back opening was draped with brown and yellow beads. The summer heat brought upon a dulled perfume of perspiration. However, Matilde was warm and vibrant. Matilde walked and smoked around the house perimeter.

Demitasse coffee was brewed and cookies were on the table. The television in the house was on and the radio blasted outside. The 'Latin' mixes were recognizable. Between the flight, time change, and the *Daddy Yankee* song coming through the speakers, I had to fight the desire to close my eyes. Mate was the stimulant shown. In the background, the parrot was speaking and Nicola was left inside in his wheelchair. Crates of suitcases filled with pictures were brought out and placed on the patio table. Photographs were taken of the photographs. With each picture shown, a story was told. Matilde was not speaking in complete thoughts or in English. She spoke in Argentinian Spanish. Her daughter, Lucy, would translate her mother's words and thoughts to English. Later, Matilde conveyed that her other house was in the process of being built. It was located down the road. The workers were creating a two-family house that would be livable--with an upstairs and downstairs area. She exclaimed, *We have a beautiful house…but when I come here in 1955, nothing.*

Finding Patterns

In the backyard of Matilde's old house, the back opening that was used for an entrance to the house was draped with brown and yellow beads. An ornament hung from outside. It said, "Home." The window next to this frame had metal bars on the outside. On the inside, a curtain covered the bar. The linens had an airy feeling. Wooden chairs and tables were scattered on the patio outside. When someone passed through the beaded-draped opening, they entered the kitchen. The table was pushed up along the side wall. The sink and refrigerator were against the opposite wall. There was an ironing board in the kitchen. The housekeeper was ironing in the kitchen.

A computer was placed in front of the kitchen table alongside the corner wall. Glass and wooden closets held an array of cups, saucers, glasses, and dishes. The items could be seen through the transparent glass. A large screen TV was placed next to a dining table. On top of the TV were framed photographs. Each room had multiple activities. There were mostly framed photographs in this house. She, too, had a china closet with dishware from New York. On another mantle in the common room were statues of holy figures.

In the bedroom, Matilde pointed to the pictures on her dresser. One picture was of her child whom she lost at birth, and the other was of her deceased sister-in-law. *This was Pasqualina. My sister-in-law...if she live today, I'm no here. I stay in New York.* She shared that she was very close to her sister-in-law when living in New York. Her sister-in-law passed away of cancer.

Matilde was now having another house built. Her house had taken almost a year to be completed. Lucy indicated that from month to month there were enormous developments and improvements. Through our conversations, Lucy had accounted for every detail. The kitchen cabinets required installation and the carpenter needed to finish the customized closets. Lucy conversed with Mariano, who was responsible for the wooden floors. He said perhaps they would be able to move in sooner than expected.

At a time when Matilde had stayed in post-war Italy, this final move in her life was by choice, and she was modernizing her living space now. Movers needed to be called, and the timeframe was on Matilde and the builder's schedules. Particular pressures came with designing a home and then taking all of one's belongings into a new space. There was an art to the design and procedure.

They believed this move would be their last move. The anxiety revolved around time and "getting things done." Lucy would run down a list of work to be done. The requirements included having the house painted, assembling the bathroom vanity and toilette, and making contact with the electricity specialist and his full crew to install all the lighting fixtures. To beat the heat in January, central air and the heating were being tested.

The electrician and plumber handled the more immediate moves, like a separate shut-off system for the Jacuzzi or climbing up on the roof to install the motor for the air extractor on top of the stove.

As the weather changed, Lucy factored in that each of these systems needed to be in-tact. The arrangement of furniture and the curtains around the house windows needed placement. Time was needed for them to shop and coordinate the décor. Considering the electrical line with the phone installation could be difficult when receiving wireless internet. The signal was only received upstairs in the guest room. The house was made of all brick, and the signal did not disperse throughout the house. This also impacted telephone calls. This was the role of the electrician and his crew because they planned to make one entrance from the outside. Through this entrance, they were going to run the cables through the walls in the same slots made for the cable TV. It did not make sense. Frustration mounted as Lucy waited and managed the current house and cared for her two aging parents. She would laugh with relief. It was an inconvenience when the phone rang, and they were downstairs. She could only speak on the telephone in Matilde's room. Arranging a house can become a comedy of errors.

Matilde's home and family were in transition. Lucy took a thoughtful approach when mapping out the development of their home. The detail to where the phone would be situated and where people may be communicating in the house were schematic. A repeated word that Lucy commented on was the essence of "time." The temperament was a concerned feeling of pressure. There was attention placed on the heat and plumbing issue. It gave Lucy angst because it would not be finished before the seasonal shifts. There were connections to the placement of where her father and mother would be in the new household. Lucy was responsible for the decision making process and all of the stages of the house's development.

On one of the last days that we visited with Matilde and her family, we entered the backyard of Matilde's old home, and the smell and sight of smoke could be found blowing in Matilde's face. She was wearing a red apron and barbequing a large array of meats. The meat was in different shapes and sizes and had varied layers of thickness. The barbeque sparked some fire. The fire added to the heat of the day. Matilde held a cigarette in one hand--a Corona and the phone were on the ledge of the barbeque. As she turned the meat and stood close to the flames, she would place her cigarette down and pick up the Corona. Between the temperature and the smoke from the barbeque, the heat was intense.

Another show was on the TV, and it could be heard as we dined. The noises in the background were from plates being moved around and voices from the television. Matilde, Lucy, Nicola, Phyllis, Sylvia, the housekeeper, and Veronica, their friend, sat at the table. Food was placed on the table. Phyllis asked, "What is it?" Matilde responded, *Coca*. Her daughter, Lucy followed up, "It's a vegetable...hearts of palm...like a tomato and ketchup." The language spoken was in Spanish. Phyllis watched the screen, and said smiling, "I speak English you speak Spanish so we learn a little bit." She laughed. Lucy went further in detail about the vegetables, "Too sweet...muy dulce." Phyllis replied, "I will taste it."

Phyllis continued, "We haven't seen you in a while...nice to be here." The conversation changed when referring to St. Pasquale's feast, Phyllis commented, "We love to go to that one...it brings back the family, the community." Phyllis asked about which piece of food on the table was "most popular." Lucy responded, "The mozzarella... Filomena try one with the corn...how do we call the vegetable sauce... sautéed onions...try this." (The phone rings).

Matilde turned to me *I drink a Corona...do you want wine?*

Lucy was on the phone and she responded to the voice on the other side "Si, bueno, si, okay, ciao." Phyllis asked, "Que lingue prefer?" Matilde responds, *Español*. Phyllis remarked that Pasqualina would have said, "both because she has a mouth to talk."

Phyllis asked when Lucy got off the phone, "How do you stay so thin?" Lucy responded, "Delgado explains another word for thin." (We smiled). Phyllis continued, "No how do you stay thin?" Lucy said, "Nerves, I don't eat well...I don't exercise; I run around for Nicola." Phyllis asked if this large screen television set was for Lucy's mother. Lucy responded, "Yes." Phyllis gave a suggestion, "This will look nice in that big room over there...the plasma TV."

Lucy said, "The pizza is different." Phyllis agreed, "Like Giuseppe, Pasqualina's husband... he likes anchovies...I like anchovies too." Lucy added, "Usually when you go to the pizza place...they place another slice on top of that..." Phyllis blurted out, "Oh gosh...like a double decker."

Phyllis shifted the conversation. "I can't believe everyone was landing when we were; did you have to wait long?" Lucy continued, "I wasn't sure if I was at the right terminal." Phyllis asked, "Did you check online?" Lucy responded, "They said you made up a lot of time in the air."

Lucy brought out the fruit. "They said in Miami all the fruit froze from the cold winter. I think they lost all of their strawberries." Phyllis added, "You know what it's gonna cost?" Lucy agreed. "That and the orange juice." Phyllis recalled how the dropping temperatures impacted Arizona's produce. "In Arizona...orange, grapefruit, persimmons, Susan loved to plant...she says she had a fig tree and it died. Giuseppe sent it through the mail...and it was just budding and a frost came."

We looked at the television. Phyllis commented, "What happened with that guy on the...the Christmas bomber...he's Nigerian...see, he had it in the shoes." Lucy echoed, "He had it in the shoes."

The language on the television switched to English and the channel was CNN.

Phyllis said prayers; she took a picture of all the food and began eating. There was goat—chicoli. Matilde served. *Mangia too.* Phyllis turned to Matilde, "Oh you can't eat this." Matilde was waiting for the setting to be done for her teeth. Matilde pointed to the water--*acqua* then pointed to *the beer...Coronita.*

Phyllis pointed to the meat on the table. "This was the meat we put in the sauce...you braise them." Veronica was helping us get around during our stay and she entered. "Mar de Plata."

Matilde made blood sausage. *Some are made with walnuts and raisins...this is just one.* Phyllis bit into it. "Softness of a liver." Lucy continued, "I tried liver...I can't." Phyllis responded, "Maybe it's the way you make it." Lucy explained how she made it. "I make it very small and sauté it."

"With olive oil and onions?" Phyllis asked. "It is the texture of the meat," Lucy said.

During our stay, much of Matilde and Lucy's time was scheduled around the shaping of the new home, maintaining the old home, and having time at the table.

Matilde's Recreational Time

Matilde's computer was placed in the kitchen. She often placed herself in front of the computer. On the screensaver was a picture of her niece's son who lived in Spain. She kept in contact with her family from *España*. We noticed that she played games on the computer. Some of the more frequent games that she played were *Double Down Casino Slots & Poker, Zynga Slingo, Pet Rescue Saga, Panda Jam, Pengle, Jewels of the Amazon*. The backdrop on her page was of a dangling tree in her backyard.

Matilde explained, *I can play...based on the numbers that come out. 78 tomorrow*. Phyllis did not understand what she meant. "How do you play this for New York...this is here Argentina lottery?" Matilde replied, *The numbers come out they play over...over here they play the same numbers...canasta*. Phyllis smiled and said, "My father likes to smoke...just like you...she reminds me so much of my father." Lucy looked at her mother, "She looks at the numbers...everyday...she covers her mouth." (She covers her mouth because her teeth are still missing and she is waiting for implants). The computer sounded, "New York Lottery." Phyllis watched "God bless her...Pasqualina doesn't know how to use the computer for nothing." Phyllis was still unsure as to how Matilde played the NY lottery. "How do you play NY lottery in Argentina?" Lucy answered Phyllis, "I think she reads it on the computer."

Matilde spent a lot of her time on the computer playing with numbers. She enjoyed it. Lucy also informed Matilde about this navigational tool on Google. It became a nostalgic moment as they reminisced about the familiar places that were once in their neighborhood in Queens, New York. Compared to the other women, Matilde used the computer as a source of communication with her family in Spain and as a form of entertainment.

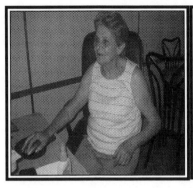 

Matilde also had Facebook. Not a new phenomenon, but she was the only one out of the four women to participate with this social connector. Her daughter communicates via email. Her other daughter, Anna, uploaded photos to her mom's Facebook page. She placed pictures of Matilde's husband's birthday party and when family from New York visited for New Year's Eve. Images from birthday celebrations came through the Facebook feed, or as Matilde call it, *a girls' party*. Skype was always on. In her new home, Matilde now had a computer downstairs in the living room. There was a collectivity among family members interacting on a social networking site. One purpose was to have distanced family members view it. Lucy informed us that Skype was an avid tool that was used in the house, and Matilde had her own computer.

If she missed some of her shows on TV, she saw highlights from a web page. Matilde played games most of the time, but also Skypes with her family in Milan and Rome and her cousin in Barcelona. Her cousin from Barcelona now came to Argentina to live with her son.

Matilde mostly communicated via Skype. When Matilde came to New York in October 2012, she said whenever a new feed came up on Facebook of anyone in New York, Lucy told Matilde to view it. *Look mommy,* Lucy said.

Matilde continued to use the computer for informational purposes and for entertainment by playing games. Lucy and her mother were up to date with the environment. Matilde in particular was afraid of the torrential downpours. During our stay there was a fierce rainstorm that made Matilde's car come to a halt on the road for two hours. The rain in Buenos Aires can be plentiful. Lucy informed us that Buenos Aires was under water that year. Areas not in Monteverde, but in Palermo and in the low--"el bajo" areas, were affected by the consistent rains. Apparently, it was the worst February in history and it already rained 49% of the 2009 total precipitations. On top of that, Buenos Aires sits over a body of water called Arroyo Maldonado (Maldonado's stream). From the beginning of the XX century, it was a project to have this stream intubated. This intubation was not done properly, and with the city's growth, now the water has nowhere to go. The current governor has been updating the intubation for quite a while, and it should be completed in 2011 and a final last portion in 2012. Hopefully, after that, it should not suffer any more floods. Airports in Buenos Aires were closed due to an ash cloud that erupted from a volcano in Chile. They were advised to stay indoors and avoid breathing in the air. The insanity of Iceland's volcano made world news as so many travelers were left stranded and isolated. Lucy discussed these informative real life events via email. This was the world in which she and her mother inhabited and came to know.

In her free time, Matilde was a catechist. She enjoyed taking pilgrimages, but she did not attend church for the holidays. In Argentina, she often went in May on retreats with her girlfriends.

Matilde headed for Tornquist with most of the ladies from the neighborhood for the celebration of the Virgin of Fatima. The six of them were assigned a log cabin, so she was pretty happy to be sharing a room with only her friends. They rested and then went to eat, and late in the afternoon, they started the ceremony and took long walks up the mountain with the procession of the Virgin. In pictures on Facebook, Matilde wrapped herself around a massive tree with friends. There was a blend between the natural world, collective spirit, and the social relationships.

We maintain our relationship through Facebook. She updated her site with pictures. She shared pictures from her husband's 80th birthday. The pictures on the site were shown to Pasqualina. Lucy wrote emails regularly. Conversations about professional soccer teams were detailed and were informative to read. She described events around soccer. This shift was a cultural transition. As seasons came and went, they were established in their home; American holidays seemed surreal and long ago. Distant past memories were sheltered in a chest full of photographs.

Over the past two years, Matilde had a few health issues and was in and out receiving medical care. Matilde had been walking a little slower, but it had not restricted her from trying to do "what she shouldn't"; so Lucy was constantly reprimanding her. Going out with her sister to the casino on Thursday nights became sort of a ritual. She reverted back to smoking. Lucy was amazed that she stopped for about three weeks and fell back into the bad habit. Matilde remarked, *I was created in a certain way and to live in that way.*

CHAPTER FOUR

Susan "Namaste"

**Don't spit in the sky; it will fall in your face
(wishing well)**
--Non sputa in cielo; che ti cado in faccia

You know I would say...the strong parts about me are the Italian parts and that little bit of loose and inquisitive--are adapted to the American side.

It was in the early 90s, after Susan's time on the East Coast of the United States, that she went to Las Vegas for vacation with her sister.

She met two women in a Vegas boutique on her vacation, and Susan decided to live there. She worked at a convention center and lived with the two women. One roommate worked as a flight attendant, and the other worked in the clothing boutique. They were considered the "Golden Girls." When Susan's mom became ill, she left Las Vegas and went to Florida. In Florida, her granddaughter, Jackie, was born. Susan has three grandchildren in Florida. She returned to Las Vegas in 1998, then Phoenix, and now she resides in Surprise, Arizona.

SURPRISE

Susan's house in Arizona has a pinkish hue on the outside. The layout of the house consisted of a kitchen, two bedrooms, living room, computer and laundry corridor, and bathroom. It was one level. Outside of the house, there were various plants. She has orange, cactus, and persimmons trees. There was a light pinkish hue, with plants surrounding the front of the house. The house shingles were wine colored. The houses on the block have an architectural consistency in makeup. Cactus plants dominate the front of the house. At sundown, the colors over the houses are reflected by the rocks. The assortments of color in the sky are white, orange, and red. It resembled the serene community. This color scheme was the design of other buildings in the Surprise development. Palm trees surrounded the Sun City Grand Community Center. The Community Center was filled with voracious conversations. People were meeting one another to sit at tables to play Mexican Dominos. Game participants were set up by the levels in which one could play.

Susan's home in Arizona contained an immense amount of artwork. The artwork in Susan's house was extensive. The guest room was comfortable and inviting. In the guest room, there was a chest. Susan said she and her granddaughter completed this project before Susan left Florida to come to Arizona. On the chest was a collage of photographs. She brought this chest to Arizona and wrapped it with plastic so the heat did not damage the priceless photographs. The outer part of the chest was a compilation of *everything over the years*. Like Matilde's chest

of photographs, each picture told a story. There was one photo of Susan's grandparents and another image of her granddaughter. There were many pictures with her three grandchildren. There was a picture of her and Danny on their honeymoon. The wooden box contained other pictures of her family. There was one of her granddaughter's mother and her daughter Theresa when she got married. There was a picture of Susan living in Vegas. She had pictures of her children when they were young. Theresa was two and her son was four and half. Other pictures included her daughter when she was a little girl and on her wedding day. She had images of her mom and dad on their 50th anniversary. She had visuals of her grandparents--her mom's parents in Italy and small celebrations over the years--*oh this was one Halloween*. She was a genie on this one Halloween. We continued to tour the house. In the guest bedroom, the picture of the Sands Hotel in Las Vegas was propped up against the wall. The guest room was dressed with silk sheets. The pillows displayed a picture of two men from Eastern Asia.

As we continued to roam the house, another portrait was of a woman holding a basket standing next to a lake. The portrait was made by needlepoint. There were trees in the background that were arching over her head. A lake was alongside of her and the willow branches formed the shape of a crescent moon.

In the living room, a modest chandelier hung from the ceiling. Below the chandelier, the dining room table held two large candle stick holders with two pink, thick candles. The glass mirror on the wall reflected the largo that was on the counter. In a circular frame, there was a picture of her two children. The picture showed the two children to be about three or four years old. It was a black and white picture. They each wore a petticoat and hat.

In her bedroom, the bed was elevated, and a silk sheet hung over the top of the bed. The roof of the bed looked like it had a handkerchief/scarf laying over it. There were silk sheets on the bed. Her bedroom displayed a photograph of Jesus with sheep surrounding him. Another picture was placed in a round frame. The picture was of her daughter on her wedding day. Another picture was a hand-drawn portrait of her granddaughter, Jackie, when she was in a beauty contest. She appeared to be about three or four years of age. Another painting illustrated a girl looking out multiple windows. The vantage point showed the girl to be looking out one window in particular. Behind her was a pew resting against the wall. The arch of the hallway where the girl stood in was angular. Each of these photos held principal significance in Susan's life.

When viewing the pictures, the rooms' decor blended with the aesthetic choices. There was a balance. In the living room, there was a sofa and chairs with cushions. In the corner of the room was a statue of an Eastern influence. A book called, *World Gods and Goddess* was on the coffee table. Two bar chairs were assembled on either end of the glass round table. Books in her picture room where the computer was situated included: *Get Healthy Now! With Gary Null. Who is Gary Null?, Emotions and Your Health, Gary Null's Guide to a Joyful, Healthy Life.* [5]

Susan spoke about her artwork. The piece in the corridor was of two females dressed in carnival attire. The females' faces were painted for the Venetian masquerade. They wore joker hats. A fuzzy ball was placed on top of the hats. Gloves covered their hands. The person in the picture appeared older looking than the other. The younger person's gaze was one of looking outward and the older-looking person embraced the younger one from a distance. One hand rested beneath her cheek. Other photographs around the house were pictures of birthday parties and of Susan holding her grandchildren when they were born. In one picture, her grandchildren's faces were painted. Susan's arms were tightly wrapped around them.

Susan was laid up in the hospital during the summer of 2012. Susan spoke further about the importance of the pictures in her house. *As to my favorite wall art, each time I acquired one it became my favorite, especially each one having a particular memory. The flower garden lady was my first needlepoint work and during a time in my life I needed to get up from a slump. The theatrical clown was from a visit to Venezuela with Randy, the kids and his wife. The Sands composer of the Rat pack singers reminds me of my time while working and having fun in Vegas. Jackie's portrait, I will always cherish. If I was to narrow it down, I should say needlepoint lady and Jackie.*

Susan's house reflected her personality and life. The portraits held layered meanings that connected to Susan's identity. The aura and energy in the house were fluid. The language and tone Susan spoke and wrote in were rested. The images depicted memories and Susan surrounded herself with these memories.

Susan cooked almost every night for us. There was clarity to the food that Susan made. The ingredients that she included in each of the dishes were purposeful and thoughtful in preparation. There was a correlation in her planning of the meal and the activity of the day. After a yoga session, she made frittata--an egg omelet with vegetables. She cut up a mango and fresh kiwi, and served the meal with whole wheat breads. After this meal, we had a tremendous amount of energy for the day.

Susan's home mirrored the color scheme of Arizona's mountainous terrain. The landscape matched the landscape in Airola. It appeared that your past did not escape you. There were parallels which have consciously and subconsciously influenced Susan and the other women. In Arizona, the dimensions of the roads appeared precise. The desert air and trees resembled a home. We were warmed by the sun while sitting in her backyard. The backyard was filled with rocks. Orange trees were in the background. Susan tried to use the seeds that Giuseppe sent her so that a fig tree could take root in the Arizona climate.

Susan started a fire in the fire pit. On top of other rocks on the side of the pit, she laid out necklaces that she made. This was her hobby. She even took a class in making jewelry. Her backyard was surrounded by plants. It resembled the description that she painted of her grandfather's garden in Italy. There were a variety of fruits. There was a patio awning and vines coming down the columns. We sat on benches that surrounded the fire pit. We sat and spoke for a few hours. The fire kept us warm, and the atmosphere was tranquil. In February of that year, Arizona had freezing cold weather at night. Most plants were anticipated not to survive that year. Susan covered them most nights.

Susan said, *If you want to eat good, eat at home.*

There was a relationship between Susan's preparation of the food and the arrangement of it. Mangos, cheeses, olives, and mozzarella balls were placed on the table during an afternoon of wine tasting. Susan explained the purpose of how the cheese accented the wine. Hanging in the kitchen was the function of an olive. It was called Huile D'olive (Bonnonne) depicted with an image of a jar, Salade Les Fils d'Emile, Huilier, Bouteille en Verre, Olivier (olive tree), and the machine of breaking down the olives (Broyeur u olives). Each evening she made us a homemade meal.

One night the menu consisted of fish, sweet potatoes, vegetables, sprouts, which included the acidity of an orange flavor. It was a colorful plate. It can be argued that our least favorite meal was the dinner eaten out. Susan did not cook Italian often. She did for the holidays. She makes more of the typical "American meal." *Back then*, she explained there were three food groups. She believed you cook and do not buy it out of a can or box. She would hope that her family would never completely drop its Italian heritage. They became a generation of the future because she believed this country had become the building block of so many nationalities, and *it got looser*. Some changes were for the better, but a lot of the traditions were lost from the transition.

Susan elaborated upon her relationship to food: *Food--there's a connection to body and soul and family and friends...more of a connection to body because of a Hindu relation...taking food in is to feed your body and soul, and you honor it and bless it and savor it...not just sitting to a meal.*

Phyllis followed up with "in the Italian family, it's the same way. You never sat on the couch; you always sat at the table. You cook with your heart." Susan responded *at my mom's house, you go visit and out comes the provolone, salami, wine;* and it is in Italy she remembered the same hospitality. After her grandfather died, she and her mother were living in this big house. On Sundays, she would go to her other grandparents' house. Her uncle and his wife, all the kids and everyone would be seated at his big table, and they would have a Sunday night supper together.

BECOMING A YOGI AND LEARNING ABOUT THE VIRTUAL WORLD

I was living in Commack and got up one early morning and turned on the TV. I saw somebody doing yoga and saw what it was. The person was doing postures and I did not know what it was; and it's yoga and I thought to myself...I wanted to do that. She was my first inspiration. Lillian Solano—

With no excuses, Susan continued to practice yoga. She continued by following yoga programs on TV several times a week. She was living in New York, *and New York City was filled with yoga studios and all kinds of places. There was a health store across the street. A sign read, "Go to Guadalajara, Mexico."* Phyllis smiled, "Did you go?" Susan continued, *Yeah, I did* (she smiled widely).

Susan was in New York and she was working, but she wanted to experience this adventure. She signed up and a yoga instructor put a group together. Susan was in her early 50s when she went on this trip to Guadalajara, Mexico. She and the group exited the plane, and a man picked them up, and he drove a van for about three hours with the yogi trainers. Susan could hardly hold back as she blinked her eyes and said, *Now it's Rio Caliente, the river--the hot volcanic river water that runs through the place.*

Phyllis asked, "You weren't afraid?" *Yeah, no I was very trusting, it was a yoga group...I like yoga.* Phyllis, quickly asked "fearful?"

Susan responded to the idea of fear not in the context of war, it was *different though, I wanted to do it.* She experienced the Hindu lifestyle twice a day. She absolutely enjoyed the yoga retreat. They had to take a search light when going from the lecture hall to the pool area, to the river, and to the sauna. They dug down and were surrounded by rocks. In the morning, they would go down to the organic water area.

She came back from Guadalajara and enjoyed the trip immensely. It drew her back to wanting to practice yoga. She wanted to learn more and signed up for a course that was being advertised on a sign in a luncheonette. She then traveled up in the mountains in California, and she participated in another yoga community practice. Each day for two and a half weeks, they learned the anatomy of the body and the fitness field. Some nurses took part in the sessions. They had the intention of pursuing it as a career, and Susan had no idea why she was there, but she wanted to learn. She was not clear on what she wanted to do. She said that her certificate was not complete without taking part in an internship, and she could volunteer. She volunteered at the YMCA by contacting the director. So every day, at a certain time, she met with fifteen people who were licensed by the State. Susan had attended either a stroke victims' unit or *some kind of rehabilitation--where the group of people either lived at home with parents and kids so they had senior day care.* She remembered one time that the session was so deep. One woman was there with very little mobility and suffered from Alzheimer's. Susan noticed that the leader organized the patients in a circle and said Susie was coming. Everybody was trying to move their foot and whatever they could get them to move, and this one woman would not look at Susan. Whatever tension she had was from within. Susan instructed her to stand up and said, *How does everybody feel today? I don't feel so good and I really need a hug. Could I get a hug?* Susan went up to this woman and she was crying and she felt her energy. She whispered, *"It's okay to cry, that's okay, let's cry today so we feel better."* It was a touching moment for Susan.

Susan's level of learning and her ability to take risks at the age of 50 was commendable. There was a progression within her experiences. She pursued her interests. She embraced opportunities during her middle age. She continued to pursue techniques in healing so that she can pass her warm energy onto others.

Susan communicated how she began her practice and her initiation into yoga began. Susan was committed to a genuine spirit of body and mind. She looked to 'Hindu concepts.' She did not find fear in meditation. She also found strength within herself. Through yoga, she had a growing sense for learning.

At eighty Susan continues to practice yoga and live the Hindu lifestyle. She spoke about the *Hindu concept--the Mother Goddess as*

Shakti. She is the origin of all creations. She is all that is divine and abundant. Shakti is the source for energy, which symbolizes LOVE, COMPASSION, CARE, DETERMINATION, CAPABILITY and to protect that which is love.

At the end of 2012, Susan fell and broke her shin. She was laid up in the hospital, and rehabilitation followed for several weeks. Shortly after the surgery, she began instructing her classes; but she still was not able to engage in every pose properly—slowly she would get there. She was confident in herself. She felt lucky and blessed for the recovery. Susan included statements about her physical ability. The strength in her muscles were cut down and compromised. She was grateful for the social aspect during her recovery. She continued saying that her friends were tending to her garden. She included the "Lord" in her gratitude. She explained what the doctor saw in her x-ray. In a phone conversation, she expressed that it was difficult to eat the food served to her in the rehab place where she was receiving treatment because it was not in her personal diet plan. She discussed her daily activity and physical therapy process.

Susan was a devoted friend. In 2011, she phoned from Arizona to inform us about airport delays as we traveled to Argentina to visit Matilde. Susan called and left a message on my cell phone. She said, *I was just watching TV on the news. It is 1:15 p.m. over here and they say the Atlanta Airport has a lot of delays and since you are not answering you must be on your way…have fun, love you, goodbye.* We still keep in contact by phone and through email. When emailing Susan, she commented on how she was managing to open an attached Word Document. (*This is the way the email appeared).

what am i doing wrong? when I put the curser on the line it does not allow me to accept typing, if I open the document first it is opened into office but click to open comes a blank, sorry for my, ignorance, Susan ps if you call me maybe you can walk me through oh,, that love computer, frustrating when I cannot do certain things, but i seem to learn a little bit each time I incur a problem

Susan included her distress about the functions of the computer, but she was willing to ask for assistance politely and proceeded. Susan is motivated to experiment with the computer and the cell phone. She gradually became familiar with the tactile movement and the understanding of its features. She noticed parallels between the computer and cell phone. She recognized errors she made with the computer and the cell phone, but learned and used 'a hands-on approach' or experimented with it. She asked her grandchildren for assistance so that she could continue to communicate with them.

Her computer trials began when she was a purchasing agent. She was most familiar with a calculator in the 1970s. It was not until she moved to Florida that everybody started using the computer. She perused the internet and went onto 'love at aol' and would see if she was connected. She was more inclined to want to use the computer and learn. She signed onto a guest server at a friend's house, until she purchased her own home computer in the house. All she knew was 'love at aol'. She smiled expressively as she continued to tell of her digital experience. *You would see all these pictures and could communicate with people and then I would learn to send email*, and she mastered these tasks as she self-taught herself. But, she never cared to go much further than that. She was not interested in doing more until she moved to Arizona. She learned about researching ideas and websites.

Phyllis (smiled*)*. "Isn't that something…you moved here five years ago and you learned all that"—The touch of a computer to a novice person, *feels foreign,* Susan said. She remembered moving the mouse and wondering where the mouse was on the screen. It was hard in the beginning. Then advancement in technology introduced her to digital cameras; so finally, Susan and her friend were going together to Fischer Electronics, and her friend explained to her that she needed to buy a particular model number. Susan agreed. While they were there, they bought a colored printer. Her grandkids came the following summer and the kids took pictures. Susan was perplexed. She said she did not want the pictures on the camera; she wanted to touch the pictures. She settled for enlarging the pictures on the computer.

Her grandson showed her, and Susan loved this moment of being hypnotized by the pictures on the screen.

She admitted that she was still not as skilled and stumbled at times. She asked why she could not view certain pictures, but then had many "ah ha" moments as she worked diligently at it. Susan and Pasqualina learned to drive when living in New York. Filomena and Matilde did not. However, Susan, was more adventurous in her driving travels. Since she drove alone and would forget how to get back to her home in Arizona, she invested in a GPS. *I would always get myself lost, and I felt stupid; why do I always do that. I would feel embarrassed with myself.* She used to pick up her grandchildren from the airport. She considered calling the shuttle, but she put in her home address and the airport address, and the GPS directed her. The GPS was telling her to continue onto *Sky Harbor Blvd*, and in her head, she does not know where the heck she is. Susan struggled to get out of the airport. The GPS "Home" button guided her. She was a map person and a letter writer.

Susan's grandchildren live in Florida. They visit with her each summer. She planned activities for them and offered them advice. Often it was relational. She believed that by *choosing a partner well, together you become a building block for the next generation; and you have to make certain to have a give and take with your partner without being pushed around or abused. You have to genuinely be a part of that.* She began telling a story about her grandson in college. At the time he was dating someone. She wrote him a letter and in a round-about way she told him *that you do not know yourself all that well and you are not capable of knowing the same person that well so you are not capable of connecting on the same level. You are at the point in your life and you need to explore.* Susan was nineteen and did not complete high school when she was married, but from her observations--these "kids" get hooked too soon. They get into a mess and from her experience, her marriage was *a good one* and she was happy in it. She could have chosen differently; however, she and Danny missed out by starting with a family and house right away, and she does not advise that until the couple is financially set. Although back then marriages were put together or match made. *You get this emotional attraction when you are young and you think that is all that it takes.*

She wrote to her grandchildren. She would even mail packages, and then she tried email. But, her grandchildren did not read email anymore. *Gosh, what the heck...how am I going to stay in touch with you kids.* First they said you have to learn email, and Jackie taught her to be on the *buddy list*. Susan knew she was online and so she did that, and then 'aol' went out of style. She does not use 'aol' anymore. Now, it is text messaging on the phone. All she wanted to know was *how am I gonna get in touch with the kids when I first came to Arizona.* Susan thought it silly. Another expense--a cell phone. She liked the land line. Her grandchildren encouraged her. She agreed to buy a cell phone. She did not like all these phone prices. She thought to preload the phone with twenty dollars, but she ended up purchasing a phone from Virgin Mobile. Susan thought she would never use it. She did not intend to use it in the car, but if she was in the car and was stuck, then she could use it. However, she did not predict that the kids would start to call her on the cell phone, and *the thing beeps* and she did not know how to get into it, and it was so frustrating. *I had to figure out how to read these stupid messages after I missed them.* She kept pressing buttons to retrieve messages. She could not remember her pin number. Then she had to call Support Tech to gain access to her pin number. Once she got her pin number, she was able to check her messages. As she was fumbled through the phone to figure out options, she identified her Contacts and an Inbox for messages. She followed the instructions and hit the button. Names appeared and she attempted to send a text message to her grandson. When she saw the blinking cursor in a blank space, she determined this was where to type the message. *On the phone they have regular computer things, like a keyboard.*

She had asked how do you type "v." The old phones became time consuming and a *pain in the neck*. The letters on her phone began to wear out, and she did not know which ones they were. At the end of her first text outreach, she gets the blinking light and wrote back *'Awesome.'* She said she can do this now. She can get it right sometimes, but not all the time.

Susan spoke of how she was not given a *vision* for the future other than the little exposure she saw in her Italian community and what her father *hoped* for in another country--America. There lacked a concrete frame of reference or model of another lifestyle for Susan, Pasqualina, Matilde, and Filomena. A prescribed "vision" was that Susan would marry and have a family. She would know how to sew and knit. Education was valued within her family, but in other Southern Italian families, education would not be equitable among the entire family. There would also be limitations as to the level in which the women would receive formal education.

Susan stated that *Education broadened her knowledge and horizons. One thing I can think of...was you can see a college degree is something and I did not have one but I did have my broad wanting to learn about things...mine is more practical experience, more people experience... every place I lived you get to know about people about how they think. I encourage young people, to live their life.*

CHAPTER FIVE

Pasqualina's Garden, Whole Food

**If you don't listen to your mother or father,
you find yourself in a hole that you
don't know how you got there**
--Chi non ascolta a mamma e padre
si trova un fosso che non sape

I am Italian and I live in America... I am an Italian American.
    Pasqualina and her husband have been living in a house in Wantagh, New York for over thirty-five years. They refurbished the house after moving from Woodhaven. The entire front of the house is brick and

stone. The front part has larger bricks that provided a sandy base. The outer perimeter and backyard resembled a typical brick layering approach of assorted colors of maroon and dark greys. In the winter, the fig trees were covered with black garbage bags, yellow rope, and white buckets with a silver handle--the bucket has another function in the summer. The backyard was bare, and the dirt was covered with long planks. The greenhouse Pasqualina's husband built was made from used middle school pentaglas windows. It houses most of the other trees that decorated the yard in the summer. Inside the shed there was a wooden wine-making presser along with many glass jars for preserving wine, mushrooms, and homemade sauce. In the summer, the trees sprout figs. Other trees in the front of their house include lemon trees, olive trees, and cactus plants.

Her husband sometimes would burn his papers in a metal trash basket amongst the garden. As the ashes blew away, Pasqualina would shout out to him to make sure the fire was contained at a low flame. She did not want the police to see the smoke. You could bring the materials you owned and have them burned. Pasqualina's husband would initiate to pour the items into the metal can. He watched and maneuvered the stash with his rod stick. The black smoke filled the air and the fire was mesmerizing. In the silence, there was a mutual understanding.

As you continue into the house, there was a "gender divide" --a split level ranch. A screen door allowed for entrance into the top level of the house. There was a glass china closet and dining room table. The table has a glass covering with wooden pegs. On each tile on the floor was a flower. The flower was auburn with green vines. This room was connected to the garage; the garage held a maroon Cadillac and many of the same types of plants and herbs that the greenhouse would hold. Since it was winter, sausage, hot pepper and garlic cloves hung from a yellow rope. The rope ran along a horizontal string. On the other side of the dining room, between the dining room table and the kitchen, there was a glass door and a wall acting as a semi divider. It looked like a diner set up because there was an open window within the wall space where the sink was connected to on the other side. Plates can pass through the opening so the plates could be set on the ledge and then placed on the dining room table. Pasqualina's china closet was in the dining room. Plates that she received from her 25th Wedding Anniversary and glasses which were given as favors from other weddings were placed.

On the other side of the divider was the kitchen. The kitchen table was wooden and square. Whenever we have coffee or dessert, or essentially anything, a tablecloth was placed on it. The remainder of the kitchen was narrow. The sink was on one side and the stove was on the other. Cabinets surrounded the bottom and lower areas.

The refrigerator rested next to the back wall. Pasqualina yelled, *keep the door shut,* so the food stayed cold. There was another door on the back wall. There was a stairwell behind the door. There were about twenty stairs until you arrived at Giuseppe's "man cave." In the basement area, there was an ironing board, old sewing machine, another refrigerator, sink, kitchen-like table, bicycle, bathroom, boiler, washer and dryer, and couch. When growing up, her grandchildren would play by the bar area. The trinket glasses were left behind the bar counter. The glasses were not there anymore. The less frequently it was played with, the more cobwebs formed. The memory of the smell of Giuseppe's Marlboro 100s cigarettes permeated. The ashtrays on the coffee tables and the smoke were relaxed. There was a bathroom that could only be used for emergencies because it had a "light flusher," and there was another storage closet next to the television. When the door opened, the deep interior closet was deathly dark. A metal chain hung from the ceiling. When pulled on, "la luce" appeared. When entering the closet and turning in a complete circle, it would give a panoramic view of several glass jars aligned against the walls. Most of them were "skinny bottles" with tomato sauce. There were also "plumper bottles"—mason jars which had smashed tomatoes with basil preserved in it. These bottles laid in the cool unlit closet area. The bottles sat on cement shelving. The basement was "grandpa's space" or referred to as "downstairs." There were now three televisions and no bar area.

Upstairs, next to the kitchen was the den/living room area. It had a master chair, glass table, couch, and two glass china sets. There were two large portraits hanging on the wall with several other pictures on a mantle. At the center of the mantle were Pasqualina and Giuseppe's 50th Wedding Anniversary picture. There was another main portrait of their family from about twenty years ago. It included their three children. Plants rested next to the windowsill in the den. Many of the plants "have been saved." When a plant looked like it was dying, it was brought to Pasqualina's house so that it could be revitalized. As you continue to walk through the living/dining room area, to the left was her son's bedroom, next to his room in the corridor was a mirror, then there was "nonna's room", the bathroom and Pasqualina's master bedroom. "Nonna's" room" was the room Pasqualina's mother lived in before she passed. The door was kept closed throughout the year, and in the winter, it was cold and served as a kind of greenroom. In Pasqualina's main bedroom there was one window. The furniture was wooden. There were a chest of drawers, a long armoire, and another closet. There were pictures on the dresser and a mirror above the drawers. Pictures on the drawers included Pasqualina's parents when they celebrated their 50th anniversary. There was a picture of Saint Pasquale. Also, a picture of Filomena's and Giuseppe's brother, Tomaso, who passed away during WWII, hung on the wall next to the bedroom. In the picture his brother is wearing a blue sailor's uniform. This was the same brother Filomena spoke of in having "a good head on his shoulders." A fan hung over the ceiling of the bedroom with a chain dangling from it.

Pasqualina's house was busy over the years. She had people visiting frequently. When they came to visit, she would explain their relation and association. They sat at her kitchen table and spoke the Italian language from her southern region. As a break in their conversation would occur, they would turn to Pasqualina's grandchild and say, "Didn't your grandmother teach you Italian?" The grandchild would grin and wish she knew more than how to count to ten and greet people. But learning the family's language was not encouraged.

Over the years when Pasqualina spoke about Susan, it was as if she were a movie star. She was glamorous. She lived in the city and owned an Au Bon Pain Bakery. Or when she spoke of Filomena, it was about her large breasts that engulfed you when she hugged you. Or she would tell stories of her friends in South America, like Matilde. Wherever you traveled, Pasqualina had a friend nearby for you to call and visit. While you may grimace and say, "I do not know these people and I don't want to go see your friends," when you visited, you were glad you broke out of the social nervousness and met these hospitable migrants.

In 2012, Pasqualina dipped her wounded leg into a cool pool. She would make direct remarks about the loss of her friends. Some of her statements were prompted by the events in which were relative in the present. She vocalized her feelings. Pasqualina attended her godchild's wedding in the summer of 2012. Her godchild was the child of her best friend, Marie, from the sewing vocational school she attended in *New York*. She passed away from breast cancer over thirty years ago at the age of fifty. When she was talking about the wedding, she revealed, *I felt Marie was there*. As she continued in the conversation she expressed, *All of my friends are dead, it is sad…the sewing ladies.*

Pasqualina visits the dead religiously in the nearby cemeteries in New York. She also participates in weekly trips to the seminary with her female church friends and prayer group. She retreated with them to Our Lady of the Shrine in eastern Long Island. She affirms, *It makes me feel good* when she participates in these types of activities.

Master Chefs and the Purity of Homegrown Food

It was July 2012 and Giuseppe turned eighty in May, and Pasqualina turned eighty in October. They have been making tomato sauce all of their lives. The players at the table may have changed, but the practice continued. Sauce would be distributed after the production process.

Every August, Pasqualina and her husband, Giuseppe, would set up a production for sauce making. After the winter in New York, Giuseppe dug up his backyard and planted seeds so that a garden could grow. Giuseppe cultivated the garden in June. During the beginning of August, tomatoes were beginning to ripen. Sauce making took place in August beginning at 7 a.m. Tomatoes were ripe, and placed into a heated (capo gatto) so that the tomatoes softened. The sauce machine would separate the tomato peel and the soft interior of the tomato. The inside of the tomato would be made into sauce. A few metal pots were on a burner. Tomatoes were in a hot pot of steamed water. The air smelled like smoke. Duties were distributed. Phyllis would wash sauce bottles. When she was alive, Pasqualina's mother's role would be to place the basil in each empty bottle of sauce. Grandchildren would now wash and drain freshly grown basil. After the tomatoes softened, they went into a machine so that the tomato became a thick liquid. The sauce was placed into a long sauce bottle. Basil was placed at the bottom before the liquid filled the bottle. After the sauce was poured, more basil was placed at the top. Giuseppe would then cap the bottle with a bottle cap device. It would be placed into another metal machine so that the bottle would be tightened. This process was repeated throughout the month. This was the summer season. Everyone joined in the picking of the tomatoes, the process of creating the sauce, and finally, enjoying the sauce throughout the year.

Each of the four women made their own sauce. Depending upon where they were living and the climate, the actual process could shift. It shifted according to the number of tomatoes that were grown that year and the equipment in which they used. Over the years, gardening methods became strategic. The seeds were planted in another area. The tomatoes were more abundant depending on how the winter and spring seasons fared. As Pasqualina and Giuseppe grew older, they also had to reduce the size of their garden so that they could maintain it properly—food was never wasted.

Wine Connoisseurs and Viniculture

Giuseppe made his own greenhouse. He created a greenhouse from public school windows that were being thrown away. He built a greenhouse to store his plants and herbs during the winter months in two heated "shacks." He would order and use California grapes to make his own wine. Next to his greenhouse and in his shed he would keep an old wine barrel that churned grapes. He made red and white wine during the early part of October. He would use the wine for cooking, drinking, and gifting. Wine making in Italy with Filomena, Giuseppe's sister, was a daily ritual. Filomena's husband, when he was still alive, attended to farm activities. He grew grapes. Vines would stretch across their garden. They have a wine cellar in their home. They were very proud of their wine production. While Matilde and Susan did not make their wine, they were avid wine drinkers and knew the type of ingredients in the wine. At lunch, they both chose the wine to go with the meal in order to bring out the flavors.

Organic Tastings

Picking vegetables from Pasqualina and Giuseppe's garden was like "shopping in a supermarket." Their "supermarket" was cultivated prior to the creation of any chain "whole food" store. The garden was ideal. It was healthy and cost effective. Many vegetables were grown. There were eggplants, zucchini, potatoes, tomatoes, cucumbers, string beans, broccoli rabe, garlic, lettuce, and onions. Seeds were mailed to their home from Filomena in Airola and Susan in Arizona. Pasqualina would reciprocate and send seeds to them.

Any time we went to Pasqualina's house she would voluntarily make a salad with lettuce and tomatoes and add oil and vinegar. She would then season it with salt and pepper. The vinegar was homemade and a little bitter. She gave her freshly grown vegetables, lettuce, and figs to everyone. This practice was universal in each of the women's homes. Anyone who entered their homes would eat the vegetables of the season. The act of sharing vegetables was common.

When your kids eat, you get full too, Pasqualina said while grinning. When you enter her home, the house smelled like her cooking. Her family was so important to her. *Family is important...because it is tradition...to your kids...how do you say-* "Italian heritage." This phrase "Italian heritage" was an understanding that Susan also hoped her grandchildren would hold onto as they live. Pasqualina related food to family. She felt her job was to feed her family and nourish them well.

I value family.... I don't want my children to go through the war...more independent...society has progressed more in education...I can see it...when people go to school they sound better.

Pasqualina turned eighty as her grandchild completed her doctorate; Pasqualina was the only person in her immediate family to receive a high school diploma, and her grandchild was the first person to receive a Ph.D. in her family. When you speak with Pasqualina, it would be at the table over a cup of espresso. She said, *I always thought it was so important for my girls to be educated.* She was referring to her daughters, and education in her eyes was going to college.

Pasqualina Ruggiero is now over the age of eighty. She was a granddaughter and daughter and a mother and grandmother. She has had an incredible impact upon lives. Her daily routines were busy. Practical morning activities were dissimilar on the spectrum, but there were overlaps in philosophy. Pasqualina could be found cleaning and washing the vegetables from the garden—depending on the season, and cooking a well-prepared meal.

It is important to feel and have Pasqualina's presence. She would speak metaphorically and not realize the meanings to each of her idiomatic expressions. Her natural dialect flowed effortlessly. Pasqualina often recited idiomatic expressions from her upbringing. The most repeated phrase heard were to young females *Chi l'uomo credo paradise non vedere* (She who believes a man will never see paradise). It served as a straightforward and stereotypical idiomatic expression for a young Italian girl so that she was to have standards and not to be misled. In other words, do not let emotion or desire sway your mind's view or the values you were taught.

Her home was a place of refuge. You ate, slept and relaxed. When speaking with her, she would say, *Go lie down in my bed. I'll wake you up when you need to go.* Or *she'll just hold and hug you,* and say, *you need my touch.* Pasqualina lived by her own doctrine and code. On birthdays she would gift her grandkids with wrapped vitamins, calcium pills, and jarred marinated mushrooms, that she made. To cure a cold or flu, she advised combining lime juice, honey, and whiskey. Pasqualina and Filomena believed that to cure headaches, insomnia, depression, narcolepsy, or anything that may be bothersome, they needed food and vitamins, physical affection, and attention. *If you do not have your health, you do not have anything…You gotta be your own doctor.*

Most of the time, Pasqualina communicated daily with her family through a phone landline. She was accustomed to writing and sending Christmas cards to her friends. Pasqualina was not too open in learning how to use a cell phone. She would attempt to use a cell phone to speak with her family if she needed to do so. Pasqualina had a cell phone which she used for emergency purposes. She could read a text message, but rarely would text message using her cell phone. She did occasionally make calls on it. Unlike Susan, Pasqualina was adamant that at her age there lacked a purpose in knowing how to use a computer. *At this age… what for? I don't know how to use the phone…it doesn't sink in.* She pointed to her head. *I don't like it…that's all you do with the phone…for what? You sit at the table next to me, and you are on the phone with someone else.*

Pasqualina was not proficient with computers. Filomena, too, was not digitally motivated to learn more about technologically advances nor were Filomena's daughters in Italy. Filomena could dial a landline phone. Despite Susan pushing herself to learn and Matilde finding free time to play, Pasqualina and Filomena did not have the same will to learn about the virtual world. Filomena's husband, Pasqualino, found technology humorous. Filomena shared that one day Pasqualino was making his way to the door, and they asked where he was going. He was eighty-nine and when he went to the farm, he went alone. He did not own a cell phone. Filomena asked again, and he ignored her. Filomena responded, *La Madonna ti benedici*. (May the blessed mother bless you). He responded, "Perche viene con me." (Why she's gonna come with me). This humor invoked laughter to those at the table because this was their mindset on the idea of 'mobility'.

Filomena possessed an innocent tone during a conversation on technology. She and Pasqualina both enjoyed viewing pictures on a camera. However, Filomena had no interaction with the computer and lacked a desire to read. Her concern was more about her husband. Her response to knowing how to dial a phone number was an accepted practice, but to use a computer seemed like an interruptive practice in her home. The sound of Filomena's voice was often left on answering machines with a brief monologue. Her message on the answering machine followed this pattern: "Ciao, Chiama Zi Filomena. Abbraciasai. Ti voglio bene." (Translation: Hello, This is Aunt Filomena. Hugs and Kisses. I love you). Filomena addressed who she was calling. She identified herself. She expressed physical and emotional affection. When Hurricane Sandy occurred in 2012, Filomena was watching the news on TV in Italy and kept telephoning Pasqualina expressing her concern.

Pasqualina and Filomena's First Skype Chat

In 2010, Pasqualina had her first Skype chat with Matilde. However, in May 2012 when Pasqualina and Filomena had their first Skype experience with each other it took a week of preparation. The Skype chat was setup with Filomena's grandson, Clemente. The Skype chat allowed for Pasqualina's husband, Giuseppe, to see his sister, Filomena, for the first time in twenty years. This Skype visit turned out to be a family event. There had been only one other time after that time that Pasqualina, Giuseppe, and the family spoke with Filomena on Skype. We were celebrating Giuseppe's 80th birthday at Phyllis' house. Pasqualina's children were present with their children. We spoke on the telephone with Filomena's daughter, Sandina, and on Clemente's Facebook to confirm the time. When visiting in Italy, anything that was seen on the computer or if pictures were to be burned to a CD, Clemente performed the task.

Prior to the Skype connection with Filomena in Italy, the space was boisterous where the family gathered (a large sunroom), and we all waited with anticipation. Pasqualina fixed her hair. Giuseppe did not know he was going to see and speak with his sister. It was a surprise. He was sitting away from the computer. Pasqualina's son-in-law, said, "Ma, this is why you need a computer." Phyllis received a phone call on the landline from Italy, and they said they were going to log-in to Skype.

Clemente finally signed onto Skype. Airola still operated on dialup, and it could take longer to have an internet connection. All the women had their eyes on the computer screen. "This is cool," someone said in the background. The ring tone of Skype came on. Giuseppe poked the screen with his finger. Yells were loud. "Answer it." Phyllis said, "Come sit in this chair." The chair was located in front of the laptop. There were questions as to where to look. Pasqualina wanted to know if she looked *Okay*. The screen popped up with three smiling images. Everyone's voice elevated at a high pitch *Hey*! And we all waved. Filomena was on the screen; she wore dark circled sunglasses. Her hair was styled. Her daughter, son-in-law, and grandson were next to her. Clemente was to the side. Pasqualina and Giuseppe were in front of the computer. There was shouting at the screen. Arms were waving. The first part of the exchange offered salutations and candid jokes. *Auguri* was offered on both sides of the screen.

Pasqualina wanted everyone to be seen by Filomena. Filomena was asking to see Pasqualina's son, Pasquale. It was a sweet moment to see his face as he saw his aunt. Pasqualina kept asking, *Dov`e baby?* She was referring to Clemente's newborn child. "Dov`e a Pasqualine."

At certain times, it looked like the images and sounds were breaking up. When the screen returned, Giuseppe spoke with Clemente about the Juventus game. "*They won 3-0 nothing.*" Clemente pointed to his shirt and the hat that he was wearing, and Giuseppe waved his Italian hat and pointed to his shirt. Pasqualina continued to wave. Grandchildren sat at the screen and blew kisses. "Miss you," she said. In unison we said, "Ciao, hai una bella giornata." (Goodbye, enjoy the day).

A member of the younger generation, Clemente, asked to remain in contact via Facebook. In the message exchanges, the computer was a source that continued to build community. It was a social device and offered hands-on learning. Even if the women did not physically use the computer, they were actively engaged in viewing the images presented by other family members. This was another way to sustain friendships and connect with the extended family.

The women solely communicated with one another via a landline telephone. Matilde and Filomena used international calling cards to call across the globe. During the end of the summer of 2012, Filomena informed Phyllis that in Italy they were going to tax the landlines so that calling "regularly" would be difficult. Filomena and Pasqualina did not have answering machines. When Skype was facilitated, another medium of technology connected the women with one another and their family members. In each of the settings, family members were virtually linked and gathered around the computer to converse and see one another.

Filomena and Pasqualina do not own a computer. They have conversed twice with one another via Skype because the children assisted with the process. They also viewed pictures of their family on their grandchildren's Facebook pages.

CHAPTER SIX

Filomena's Preserve and the Culture of Airola

Open your eyes and keep your brains in your head
--Apri gli occhi e hai le cevello nel capo

Filomena brushes her hair back. She is wearing a yellow housedress. "Do you consider Italy your home country." *Si, seguro.* (Yes, sure).

Upon arriving in Airola in the summer of 2011, the first image was of an old man on a moped riding down the narrow street. He was smiling and waving his arms. This was Zio Pasqualino. His moped was an antique. We stopped in front of his house. His gestures reflected excitement. Everything seemed to resemble 1945. The weather was so hot, like in Argentina. There was no air conditioning in Filomena's house or in any of the houses on the street. There was a constant flow of smoke that filled the air. Smoke could be seen coming out of a chimney and in the distance appearing above the mountains--smoke touched the clouds without separation. It appeared nebula.

Zio Pasqualino greeted us and escorted us up the street to Sandina's house where everyone was waiting. The table was set for twenty people. She had what seemed like an assembly line of women in the kitchen. On the table were platters of antipasto filled with prosciutto, cheese, and olives. Bottles of water and wine also sat on the banquet table. Hellos and goodbyes with family became a theatrical act. Hugs were genuine and everyone held each other tightly. The night before we left, Zio Pasqualino said, "You may not find me here the next time you come." He was, eight-nine, but seven years ago, he was hospitalized, and he looked like a different person this time--thin. He was still vibrant and full of life.

However, he was correct in his statement. A few years later, at ninety-one, Pasqualino rode his moped for the last time. After coming home from the farm, he felt pain in his lower stomach. He was taken to the doctor. When they opened him up, they could not do anything further. They closed his body and sent him home. Two days later on June 25, 2015, he passed. His funeral was granted according to his wishes. He was laid out in his house. Marathon runners who he cheered on for each race ran passed his home to pay their respects. His body was taken by horse and carriage. He was devoted to taking care of the cavalli, horses.

During our visit in Italy, all our meals were grand and spectacular. Fortunately, Filomena was home from the hospital. Seven years ago, she was diagnosed with a weak heart, and her daughters tended to her needs. Passion was beheld in the eyes of these people because there was so much care and concern for their mother. This was the war baby's generation who believed in commitment and dedication to people. After eating, they showed me their backyard. It was filled with different trees. It had plums, figs, lemons, olives, grapes, prickle pear cacti, berries, artichokes and more. Chickens were in their coup.

Pasqualina was surrounded by her in-laws and cousins in her hometown. I asked Pasqualina, "Do you miss Italy?" She responded, *What for? My kids are here* (meaning in the U.S.). Her home was where her kids were.

Filomena's house was located on the corner in the town of Airola and down the street from Sandina. The street was narrow. The houses across from her house were interconnected. The outside of Filomena's house was gated with black pole spikes. Often the ritual for entrance was the bell ringing, accepting admittance, and the gate swinging open. The gate and driveway/walkway area was higher than the foundation of the house. When walking into the main door of Filomena's house, two steps were at the front entrance. The three-legged dog, from what I remembered ten years ago, was not at the front door. When taking in the wide-ranging view, the mountains in the distance encircled the home.

Two steps led up to the front door. When stepping down onto the main level in the house, pictures were seen on the walls around the perimeter of the entry room. Family portraits consisted of her children and the families who did not live in Airola. The pictures were of her daughter, husband and grandchildren, who lived up in northern Italy, near Florence. Another family portrait was of her son, his wife, and six grandchildren who live in New York. She had a china closet filled with pictures and dishes. The pictures and dishware were gifts given to her on momentous occasions. They included dishware passed down from her mother, and china given to her during her 25th Wedding Anniversary, and also a plate to remember her 50th Wedding Anniversary. A collection of wedding favors sat on the shelves.

The dining room has a long table stretching about eight feet long. On the mantle across the table was an old radio and statues of saints. Rosary beads were hanging from the mantle. Filomena's house resembled a shrine. She had St. Pasquale and Padre Pio photos on the mantle, and they were seen when you walked through the door. She took multiple visits to Padre Pio's town in the past because his shrine was in the province in which she lived. Filomena does not venture far from her home, but there was a warm connected spirit to these places that she recreated. Next to this room was a walkway. The arrangement of the pictures and artifacts were deliberate in this space. It was as if each member in the surrounding portraits in the dining space area who was not living in Airola was present at the table. The statues that were

on the mantle in this dining space reflected a spirit of peace and calmness. Filomena's belief was rooted in her faith and in these saints as
protectors of her home and part of her life.

The main room is at the forefront of the walkway. The bedroom, a bathroom, and the foyer also run along the hallway. Filomena's bedroom contained a bed, a dresser, and a portrait. The bedroom was kept tidy. There were no objects on the dresser or on the bed. There was no clutter. A stairway led to another part of the house; there was another level to the house. The next level contained a bathroom, a main bedroom, a smaller bedroom, and a living space with a pull-out couch. The bedrooms each had a dresser and a piece of furniture so that clothing could be hung. The floors were tiled. The house had spaces that could hold three families. When visiting, a neighborhood car came around, announcing over a loud speaker that the water would be turned off for a day. We stored the water from the tub so that we could have bathing water for the next day, and we were not told when it would be turned on again.

The kitchen on the bottom level was the area where the interviews took place. There was a main table with a tablecloth on it. Six wooden chairs surrounded the table. Countertops lined the perimeter of the kitchen. On the counters were fruit baskets and pitches of water. A yellow phone with a curled wire was attached to the wall. There was a doorway that led down to a wine cellar. Wine, empty glass bottles for sauce, crates, and water were kept in this cool cemented area. The bottles were "skinny" and "plump."

In the kitchen against the main wall was a sink that had no dishes in it. There was a dry rack for washed dishes. There was no dishwasher. On the stove was a demitasse coffee pot. Two pots for demitasse were used. There were other small baskets on the counter with string beans and potatoes that were freshly picked. The food was cultivated from her land. Light gleaned through the kitchen window. The window was separated by the black metal spokes from the bars on the outside. Through the window, the mountain of Taburno was seen. Her house was referred to as the "albergo"—a hotel. Any member of her family who came into town stayed at her house.

Filomena refurbished her wedding sheets from 65 years ago so the "newlyweds" in our party could sleep on them. Upon departure, Filomena "gifted" us with linens. She gave dining tablecloths to the married couples. She did not have an authentic tablecloth for all--only i *sposi*.

THE CONCEPT OF MARRIAGE ACCORDING TO THE FOUR WOMEN

During the summer of 2011, Pasqualina and her family went to Italy to attend two weddings. Academic research can feel like the start of a long-term relationship. At a certain age attending weddings becomes routine, and being a part of the "bridal party" requires a separate bank account. An Italian colleague responded about the wedding expenses in that "Those types of traditions need to evolve with the modern time." It was exciting to go to a wedding in Italy, but as a single woman, you can feel like "the other" in "traditional events." A natural question that was rattled off of one's tongue was often, "When will you get married?" Marriage, from the four women's era, was terminal and fixed. They carry these ideals that existed within their communities for over a hundred plus years.

This particular ceremony would take place in the same church that Filomena and Pasqualino were married. The wedding reception for this wedding took place at a rooftop hall overlooking the mountain top of Taburno. At the wedding, the seating chart followed a traditional form with name placements. Unmarried women kept their matriarchal last name if they were not married. Names changed in Airola and were shortened in Monte Grande, Argentina. Matilde said, *They forget when it's long.*

Filomena was a staunch traditionalist. At eighty-three years of age, she rarely left her house anymore and tended to her husband. She was asked what advice would you give young women today. She repeated the question in Italian, *Chi aveso. Che consigli*. Then, Filomena responded in Italian, *Credule, Le mamme di oggi devono imparare a criscere i figli meglio*. This is translated to mean, "The mothers today should learn how to raise their kids better...they start when they are young...troppo liberta...too much." Filomena reiterated that mothers play a vital role in their children's lives. Filomena continued, *Apri gli occhi e hai le cervello nel capo. Ho sentito ha sai cose. Quando sono piccolo...no poi assicurare a nessuno.* (You have to open your eyes and keep your brains in your head. I was hearing a lot of things. The small kids in school do whatever. You can't trust anybody). *Conoscene bene.* (You have to know them well). Filomena discussed the role of motherhood. *Start when they are small. Giovane.* She said even for young single women. When considering a mate, *Choose and choose well.*

When Matilde was asked about marriage she said it is okay to be single, but, *at a certain age* you should find someone to marry. At this point in her life, Pasqualina thought it liberating when other women did not have a husband any longer. It was like an act of freedom. *You can go anywhere. Today you don't have to get married. Marie's husband would say, Il compare mi disse che oggi le donna non e necessario di sposarsi, perche le donne e uomini lavorano. Prima era necessario per la donna a sposarsi perche non lavoravano e il marito la doveva supportare la moglie.* (The young girl does not need to get married because they work just as hard as the man works. Before the girl had to get married because the husband had to support her, but now she can support herself).

CHAPTER SEVEN

"Speak Airola" through Tradition

**If you practice with a cripple after a year,
you become deaf and blind (double defected)**
--Chi prattica con zuoppo dopo un anno zuppico e cieco

The roads in Airola are interrupted by growing weeds, inclines, and man-made bridges. Walking groups tour the mountain of Taburno where a monastery was situated. They did not reach the top, but a stray dog followed throughout the walk. Halfway through the walk, they stopped at a café to have juice and coffee. When stopping at the café, the dog waited. They passed the neighborhood cemetery. The cemetery was unattended. It had stone graves and mausoleums. The mausoleums contained several family members who had passed. Photographs presented more than two dozen names and pictures on the marble slates. Behind each name, a familial voice would recite the obituaries from memory for each person. The stray dogs followed.

What does the image of "stray dogs" mean? Literally an animal was accompanying the group while being unattached to any owner. Metaphorically, entering these streets and walking through the cemetery, these stray dogs were unfamiliar beings to visitors, but were a part of the community; and a sign that we all have "stray dogs" who follow. "Stray dogs" can be interpreted to mean patterns and maps, and "dogs" are conditioned based upon settings and behaviors. These conditions, behaviors, and even emotions were not lost, but can be influential. The "stray dogs" can also be distant or immediate memories. The four women's memories were working to recall stories and processing the impact of the stories.

Upon returning to Pasqualina's hometown, Airola served as a reminder to Pasqualina in "jarring" her memory. When seeing places in her hometown, she would often say, *Now I remember*. For Pasqualina, this moment 'inhabited her.' Her sense of consciousness was interwoven with objects that served as signs which were influential upon her memory. Susan, Matilde, and Filomena had similar experiences with their own consciousness. These memories impacted their thought processes and viewpoints.

As these women became older and negotiated spaces, they often stayed with other married couples and families from their culture who were like minded so these past practices were relevant and continuously performed. The visiting of a site or viewing of photographs from a moment in time when an occurrence was significant aided in the women's retelling.

At Pasqualina's house, the fire burned the material to ashes so that the physical existence was no more. In Arizona, we sat around the fire to converse; the fire was an aesthetic piece that provided warmth. In Argentina, the ignited fire lit the barbeque grill and cooked the meat. In Airola, the fire created smoke and left its murky impression in the sky. It also gave light during celebrations. In each of these instances, the image of fire was reflected in the homes of the women and was a consistent sign shared between each of their places. This image was natural. This sign was not the only consistent visceral signifier. Practices like producing tomato sauce, wine making, and growing fresh produce were practices that originated within their regional customs in Italy.

The way in which the women discussed the events was emotional and subjective. They invoked the self. The retelling of the past assisted with understanding the women's past 'worlds', and how they lived and came to be in the present. Burns (1991) in his article on "What is Tradition?" wrote about the past and about the dead, "For the dead, of course, are not dead at all" (p. 5). In fact, the dead are alive in these women's minds and lives.

After visiting the women, they were eager to see their stories in writing because they wanted to add to them. *I wanted to give more of myself,* said Pasqualina. In an email from Susan, she wrote, *Have you completed your research yet, well I guess you will always have projects going, love to read it when completed.* In October 2012, Matilde stated, *I want to see it;* and Filomena also called and spoke with Phyllis and stated *Bisogno di dire piu (I wanted to tell you more).* It is apropos that these women communicated these responses because the women had more time to reflect. Even as these women live in their natural spaces and homes, the culture in which they were raised was dominant.

Each of the women learned a southern dialect in their region of Italy. As they lived in other areas, they acquired other languages so that they could function and operate in their new space and location. There was a blend of languages spoken during their conversations. Language was also performed depending upon the women's audiences. The women spoke in more than one language. They spoke in another way when they called across the globe to speak with family, and they speak in their current language with those they live. For example, Pasqualina speaks English to her family, but speaks the Italian dialect of Airola with her husband, siblings, and cousins. Susan predominately speaks English. She explained that she has little opportunity to speak her language of origin. Matilde speaks Spanish—influenced by Argentinian Spanish and Spanish that she learned while working in a hospital in New York. Filomena speaks with everyone the language of her town. During the interview, she would use some English words.

Language was not the only form of communication. What is understood in Airola is the openness of hospitality, and communal living and the prescribed treatment between the genders. Position and behaviors were prescribed by gender and age. While in Italy, you were conscious of being a woman. For example, they called little women "bellezza." It was understood that a young woman would help serve at each meal. Demitasse coffee was made at the end of each meal. You were criticized for not already adding the sugar in the coffee for the men. Invitations for backyard gatherings were constants. Relatives invited us into their backyards. Ever present were these customs: home grown greens in the garden and a cement area connecting to the house. They asked us to sit at the table surrounded with benches. They asked if we wanted torte (cake). We responded politely, "No." They served sliced pieces of cake anyway. They poured wine. They asked if we wanted to go into town to have ice cream. We respectfully said, "No." As we were leaving, Pasqualina asked why we didn't go into town. *They want to show you....* Those were the four words. "They want to do..." Throughout my visit Filomena would say, *You like. You want. I get.* Three simple sentences—these lines are statements because it was never a question. The same way placing sugar in coffee determined an automatic assertion.

Tradition in Airola can be understood if one stayed and experienced the roots of the culture. Filomena's grandson, Mikey, who lived in Northern Italy near Florence, said that Filomena and Pasqualino and the family "speak Airola" because their language is inherently molded. Sometimes no one outside this esoteric group understood what the older generation was saying since the language was only known in this area. The older generation had minimal formal education in their native language so they often spoke in idiomatic expressions. It was not only their language that was not as recognizable to the untrained ear, but their practices were more meaningful to the families who lived and visited this place.

SAINT PASQUALE AND PADRE PIO

Each of these women re-enacted festivities that were native to their town. They paid reverence to Saint Pasquale and Padre Pio.[6] Filomena spoke about the feast of Saint Pasquale as a social activity; she went to *scuola, celebrated Saint Pasquale, canta (sang), and embroidered.* Matilde possessed pictures where her husband carried the statue outside the social club in the 1980s in East New York. The procession was re-enacted for many years prior and after. Matilde spoke of *the procession in the streets in Brooklyn.* Pasqualina called the feast of St. Pasquale a *tradition.* When the women were younger, they celebrated the patron saint of their town, Saint Pasquale. There would be a procession and parade. They marched behind the statue. Men and women had specific duties at the parade. The men carried the statue. The women made tartalle—dough made from scratch with fennel seed. Little girls wore their communion dresses and joined the event. The procession had taken place in the town of Airola, in Italy. In 1901, when families began to move to East New York, the celebration of St. Pasquale continued in the streets of Brooklyn, and they reserved a space to hold the St. Pasquale Society meetings. Only men were and are allowed to attend these meetings. The recreation of the parade and the annual mass takes place on Liberty Avenue, in Jamaica, Queens. Closer to the patron saint's feast day, there would be a major celebration with over 400 guests held at a catering hall. There would be food and Italian music. Each of the women had been to this event at one point in time.

Each woman had a strong connection to St. Pasquale. Susan spoke about the food and the dancing at the feast. Pasqualina sold tickets to those who wanted to attend the dinner dance and was actively involved in the event each year. She invited guests, got sponsors for a journal, and solicited raffle tickets. Filomena was committed to St. Pasquale. Her husband was named after the patron saint. She relives the festivities in Airola each year as her town celebrates it.

In each of their homes, pieces of artwork, photos, or statues of faith hold meaning. Faith in these homes reflected a sense of "allegiance to duty or a person," "sincerity of intentions," "firm beliefs," "complete trust,"[7] or a "belief in God or doctrines." In Christianity, faith differs among the various Christian traditions. Christian faith is living spiritually and believing in "God,"[8] and in Hinduism one idea of faith is, "knowledge beyond the mind..." Descriptors were included from these two religions because each of the women was raised on the belief of Christianity, and Susan had a strong connection to the tenets of Hinduism.

Pilgrimaging

Upon uttering the word 'pilgrimage', it can be agreed that there is a sense of richness to it. It holds multiple meanings--inter-textual meanings rather than assumptions that these women are simply transient wanderers with limited direction. Each of these women's journeys across states, countries, and continents, was unpredictable and purposeful.

Pilgrimage, in itself, can have a religious and/or spiritual connotation. It can be a mental and physical trek. In a literary and traditional way, pilgrimaging was often taught through the Canterbury Tales or Medieval Literature. A focus was on the search for the holy grail.[9] Buddhism, Hinduism, and Christianity do consider pilgrimages to be a journey of faith and great moral significance. The women's annual pilgrimages to seminaries and retreat places focus on time spent in natural environments and on creating a space of solitude. Their interactions in these events present the women to be calm social beings. They strengthen friendships in these circles.

When asking each of these women why they participate in these activities, each responded in a way that suggested a sense of "serene repose." It was calming. They "enjoyed" the visit and moments when they were there. They found collective support within their group. By saying a prayer or visiting a place that exhibited qualities of commitment and faith, these women believed in the ethos and spirit of the aesthetic environment.

The Sanctity of Food

You don't waste. It is a sin to waste. Pasqualina
If you want to eat good, you eat at home. Susan
What can I give you? I'll make. Filomena
This is good, try this. Matilde

Each of these lines referred to a mentality toward food. The women all grew up in a rural area in Italy during WWII. Each had experience with farming. Food was situated with a moral connotation. Susan presented it as an interconnection to the body and soul. Her reading material informed her of the function of food for later years. Filomena prided herself on her farm and in producing homemade meals. From her farm and growth of resources, many have sampled her corn, string beans, tomatoes, potatoes, wine, lemons, figs, artichokes, olives, and olive oil. Filomena's daughter, Sandina, had an assembly line in the kitchen. Three women were staffing the station in the kitchen. The meal concluded with granita--iced lemonade made from freshly squeezed lemons. This attention was given because of guests' arrival and because it was the afternoon meal. In Argentina, there was an adopted cultural understanding. Matilde did not want a guest to miss the taste or savory pleasure. The cow was considered the central source of food. We remarked that every piece of the cow was used. "So much meat was on the barbeque." "Grandma's delicacies," we said. Delicacies arrived in the form of body parts from different animals. "Ooo, tripe." Through cooking and setting time for dining, women brought family together. They cooked from the heart, and each of the women found joy in this act. By bringing family and friends together around the table, discussions and conversations transpired. Each of the foods was connected to the earth and the environment in which the women lived.

Eating and dining in the home with each of the women was unique. After eighty years of life, Pasqualina, said she was a *professional* and *knew everything*. Her concern was with who would be at the table to indulge in her abundance of food. It was understood that nothing could be wasted. Susan's background, when dining at the table, was quiet, and the focus was on the individual's voice while enjoying the flavorful details of each dish. Filomena's meals were open to extended family members around the neighboring houses. Conversations, a multitude of food, an array of people, and a number of women helping, were consistent images in this dining pattern. At Matilde's house the radio and televisions could be heard and viewed in the background. Meat was the item of consistency on the menu. The homemade food reflected what was available to the women in their region.

A friend once said to me, "An Italian mother is a sacred thing." Typically, stereotypes were formed about Italian mothers. Presentations in movies conveyed Italian mothers to be the dominant domestic housewife who cooked, cleaned, and maintained control of the house. While this may be true, they have a strong commitment to family and faith. It was important and necessary to challenge the perception of these women so they were viewed as a more integral resource for future generations.

When staying with these women, they each provided a safe, loving, and energetic environment. They were overly hospitable. Before arrival they would ask, *How many are coming?* This way they would know how many people to prepare for. When leaving, they were eager to know when we would return? *When will I see you again?* They asked.

Branding or coining these women as only "domestics" does not do them any justice. They are entrepreneurs, master chefs, wine connoisseurs, spiritual advisors and more. They are humanists and markers of hope for our future generations who will undergo change at rapid rates, and their lives will be compounded with catastrophe. The four women's tenacity is inexplicable; the image of their being is ingrained to create not a crutch, but a tank for mental strength.

GATED HOMES

At the current moment, the places visited were the residences of the women. Each of these women physically lived in a gated community. In Argentina, Matilde, and in Italy, Filomena, were exposed to kidnappings, robberies and private theft in the communities in which they resided; therefore, they gated and bolted their houses. In Surprise,

Susan lived in a community with senior citizens. In order to live in her community extensive background checks took place. Pasqualina gated herself in Wantagh in a suburban life. Filomena, Matilde, and Pasqualina were restricted in partaking in particular actions because of family obligations; and more specifically, in Susan's situation, it was the monetary restriction. The natural environments in which they each lived resembled the backdrop of Airola.

In the distance, in Argentina and Arizona, mountains bordered Matilde and Susan's homes. Pasqualina's garden reflected her farming days as a child. Filomena never left the Monte di Taburno. In these spaces, their homes and communities were the locations where they recalled their past. It was interesting that they shaped their present homes to imitate an aspect of their native homes. It appeared comforting. It could be the result of fear or nostalgia. They each recounted that they hold onto past terrors or it could be how they read the situation of their present spaces. In each case, the impact of the war carried weight in their minds.

Part III
WEIGHTED LABELS

CHAPTER EIGHT

The Weight of the Dead

The loaf of bread is breaking
--Un pane sta `e spezzando

Susan, Lucia (Pasqualina's sister), Matilde, and Pasqualina's sisters-in-law, Vincenza and Filomena, have all outlived their husbands.

In Filomena's interviews, she spoke about her brother, Tomaso, and her father. She began to say, *I gentori molto giovani (My parents*

very young). *B*oth of her parents were *too young* when they passed. Her brother was a young adult, and her father was fifty-six years old when he died. Also, Filomena's daughter, Sandina, argued that it was not right that Filomena's parents were not buried together in Italy. Her grandmother should be buried in her hometown, next to her husband. Her grandmother was buried in Long Island, NY and her grandfather was buried in Airola, Italy—down the road from Filomena's house. At the cemetery, pictures were in a frame on the tombstone. There was a picture in the frame on Filomena's father's tomb. There was an empty frame and tomb for Filomena's mother. Sandina sadly repeated, "This is not right." In the cemetery, there were many of Pasqualina, Filomena, and Susan's family members, and now Pasqualino's body and picture rest. Cemeteries in Buenos Aires and Airola were close in proximity and publicly open. This allows for 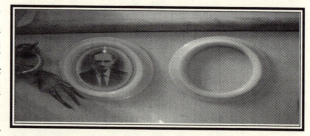 Matilde to visit her husband, Nicola's grave. We visited Evita's grave in Buenos Aires; Matilde went to her public funeral in 1952.

The names of individuals in each of these places held importance. Cemeteries had family names engraved in stone. When speaking about the dead, there was a strong sense of "the dead's" presence. After saying the name of the deceased, the phrase, "May they rest in peace," was slowly repeated. Everyone's name had a historical and familial meaning. The women would introduce individuals who were named after a grandfather or mother. By re-using the same names within a family over time, it was adding to the identity of the person who carried the name because it imposed another layer to his or her identity.

At the table, the names within this circle of women seemed to follow a pattern. Two recurring names were Filomena and Lucy. Each was named for a great grandmother in the family and after a saint.[10]

Even after saying the name, there was a descriptor indicating who they were related to—for example, Filomena e la mia mamma Nannina. Along with this apposition, each of these women also had nicknames. Addressing these women in a particular way was dependent upon where they were and who they were with. Often their birth name was adapted from their Italian name and into an English name.

FULL LIFE CYCLE: COPING WITH GRIEF

Nicola Lamberti was honored in March, 2013 at the 106th St. Pasquale feast at Russo's on the Bay in Howard Beach, New York. On Monday, May 27th, 2013, Nicola went into cardiac arrest at the outdoor table of a family Memorial Day barbeque. He was surrounded by his family—wife, son, daughter-in-law, grandchildren, great-grandchildren, family members and friends. Giuseppe so innocently remarked, "Poor Nicola, he didn't even get to eat."

Pasqualina's brother, Nicola, passed away on Monday, June 4th 2013. He was on a respirator for a week long. He had brain damage, and his wife, Vincenza, eventually took him off the respirator while their three children, nine grandchildren and spouses watched him pass.

Pasqualina and Giuseppe were at the hospital. Nicola's eyes were open, but there was no activity. He was in bed hooked up to monitors with an IV. His son and daughter-in-law were present. Many family members and friends visited all week long.

Pasqualina and Giuseppe walked towards Nicola's bedside, their dear brother, and said, "I'll see you later..."

It was a difficult time for Pasqualina, Giuseppe, and Giuseppe's sister, Vincenza. Pasqualina's brother, Nicola, was married to Giuseppe's sister, Vincenza, for sixty-three years. After the funeral, someone whispered to her "You are a strong woman." She responded, "Of course, you have to be." We can hold that direct expression as an affirmation.

Throughout this very difficult week, Pasqualina made comments, about her brother that she may not have said twenty years ago. We begin to verbalize these ideas sometimes when we grieve. It is a replay of words that could have been said.

Pasqualina convinced herself that she was not old. She said her brother had at least another three to five years. He was eighty-five years old when he died. She claimed that eighty was the new sixty. When learning of the news of her brother's passing, she made manest all day. Later in the day, she cleaned and prepared fresh-grown lettuce and placed it in a salad bowl. Phyllis was more hyper than usual. She looked like a piece of paper, frail. Nobody was eating. Relatives from Italy (sister, nieces, nephews, cousins) called two to three times a day. Filomena had her grandson arrange to put up a banner in the town to announce Nicola's passing in Airola. It served as a newspaper obituary announcement.

Lucy and Matilde in Argentina spoke to Pasqualina. She was in shock and deeply upset by the sudden loss. They spoke affectionately and with love. This generation was beginning to wonder.... the percentages of deaths were starting to rise.

Susan wrote on the online funeral home's guest book:

> June 07, 2013
> Dear Nicola, my fondest memories of our long awful trip from Italy, and looking forward to the great joy of seeing our dad, here in the US, times we never forget may the lord receive you with open arms, Vincenza, so sorry for the loss, my prayers are with you.
> Love and Peace, Assunta Rufrano

The three-week boat ride for this generation are three weeks that they would like not to recall. Giuseppe does not speak of his boat ride from Italy nor does he get on any boat of any kind after his immigration experience, seventy years later. Pasqualina began to reminisce and make comments, too, about her brother. How he was a *good brother* to her and her sister.

At the wake, all the members from the St. Pasquale Society came to pay their respects and a roll call was made silently. Prior to roll call, each of the members said prayers by the casket. During this procession two other individuals made their way between the procession. They did not realize that this was the St. Pasquale Society's moment. We knew they did not belong because one was a woman paying her respects. Giuseppe whispered, "Chi 'e la?" Nicola was the most senior member of the Society and was the former president.

The suddenness of his passing halted a wine project he had undertaken. The morning of his cardiac arrest he was setting a date with his grandson to bottle his homemade wine for his upcoming wedding. It was to be given as a guest favor. They drank to him that week. They drank the wine he made, and it was later bottled by his children and grandchildren the day after his funeral.

After the funeral, as we were gaining entrance into the cemetery plot, the fifty cars that were following the hearse halted. Phyllis exited the car she was driving and walked up front to ask, "What was the delay?" Giuseppe replied, "They have to check Nicola's passport."

After the deacon led the final farewell, Nicola's son hosted a barbeque in the backyard, which was beautifully landscaped with the help of his father, Nicola. It had a brick-made barbeque, a Tiki bar, pool, awning to deter the sun, and tables. A sister-in-law of a dear friend of Nicola, who was also honored with her husband three months prior, said we waited until Nicola was placed to rest inside the drawer. "We wanted to be sure they put the right person in his space." She spoke about how the mosquitoes were beginning to make their way inside the "capo." She spoke of the temperature in the room of the mausoleum. She explained that her drawer space was located at the bottom because everyone already had chosen their rows for their burial place. Her brother-in-law said, "I'm buried with my wife and her sister. I can't get away from their constant chatting." Giuseppe and Pasqualina were midway up. "They didn't want to be in the cheap seats when they died," said the widowed wife--and so they chose a convenient space at a higher rate for their final resting place.

In Italy, Filomena had a funeral mass said for her brother-in-law, Zio Nicola (Uncle Nick) two days after his funeral mass in the United

States. It was an evening mass. The church located in the town square was full. Many relatives attended—his sister-in-law, brother-in-law, nieces, nephews, great-nieces and, great-nephews, cousins, and other distant family members and friends from the town came.
Lucy in Argentina wrote:

> We got the call around noon with the sad news.
> So sorry, my deepest condolences.
>
> Please give my regards. You are all in our prayers, will try to speak to you soon.
>
> Love, Lucy

Nicola was a person who did not need to say many words because there was weight to the few words he said--a valuable quality. *Poco parole fa buon intendidore* (Few words make good intentions) said Pasqualina. This older generation leaves their presence by the objects they have made and through the memories of their traditions.

After undergoing tremendous trauma and significant joys over a lifetime, the four women are responsible for burying the dead, too. With a peaceful presence they are dutiful, and they undertake this task. The convictions in which each woman spoke, and the strength they carry, especially now, we, too, should adopt the ethos of these magnanimous souls.

CHAPTER NINE

The Storm

The old woman was one hundred years old and she was still learning
--A vecch era cento anni e allora si imparava

On October 30, 2013 at 5:30 a.m., the morning after Hurricane Sandy, Pasqualina's son-in-law took his jeep to work. The street to the main road was like a river, and the jeep puttered through the water. The battery died on the way. At 7 a.m., Phyllis stumbled through the streets looking for familiar faces. People trickled out from their houses with glances of fear and disbelief. Pumps were pushing water out of hoses that were linked to houses. Pumping would go on for days. Leaves were saturated—they were stuck to the pavement. Daylight came and went.

That night, we went to Pasqualina's house to have a hot meal which was bought from a local pizzeria. Her generator provided heat and light.

Phyllis, her husband, and children sat with Pasqualina's son, Pasquale and Giuseppe. They were gathered around the table. Giuseppe's deep red wine was in a carafe. He actually remained at the table for the full meal since the cable was out and there was no "soccer ball" game to watch.

Arugula salad was brought to the table. We had brick-oven pizza and grilled chicken which was picked up from the local pizzeria. The pizzeria had running generators. Pasqualina was smiling and laughing throughout the meal. She was watching us eat. We sat closely around her rectangular kitchen table. Not everyone could fit at the table, but more chairs were brought into the kitchen to accommodate the crowd. A circle formed so everyone could be seen. She told us that she was so happy that we came. She addressed everyone and said, *You know, when your kids eat you get full too*, while smiling widely.

Pasqualina took out the demitasse cups and made coffee. As it was percolating, she washed the dishes. The conversation at the table turned to laughter. She said, *It is good to laugh at a time like this…we are together here…and it's good we can laugh.*

As we were leaving, she encouraged us to stay longer. She turned to me and asked if I wanted to sleep at her house. We hugged tightly and I went home to a powerless, cold house.

The neighborhood was devastated.

The media kept saying at the time that "it was a 100 year-storm."

The hurricane left us without power. Daylight was arriving later and departing sooner. Sitting in one area of the house, with random sized candles as a source of light (conserving the batteries on the flashlights), was not a past-time. The resounding noise of beating generators was a regularity throughout the day. Policing at gas stations became a daily ritual as gas became scarce. Car lines were on the shoulders of main roads. People held red gasoline buckets. Many were turned away because the station did not have enough gas.

When driving on main roads, stores were boarded up with wood or tape. Trees were completely uprooted on all streets. Some trees exposed their roots to the road and some landed on houses. Select coffee shops were filled with communal wires.

Power in the humane sense was leveled during the hurricane. It humbled us. It reminded us that we were fragile, and not invincible against mother nature. We all experienced an event that was relative to our lives. We emotionally weathered a storm. We saw it. We felt it. We sympathized with the loss that some experienced. We saw the physical remnants left behind. We saw faces of those who will spend a significant amount of time picking up their pieces.

It became a week without power. At the end of the week, I went to Pasqualina's house for a home-cooked meal. She made homemade lasagna. When I went over, she told me *you are the last of the shift to come.* I put down my coat and bag and handed her a mug. It read "Grandmothers are just antique little girls." A plate was placed on the table, and the red sauce towered over the lasagna sheets. Ricotta and chop meat seeped out from the edges.

She said, *I made it all...the pasta shell too. All it is are flour and eggs. I went out and let it set and harden for a few hours.*

She said this as if everyone knew how to make pasta dough, and I, of course, knew the image she explained. I had watched her make dough from scratch as I had watched Pasqualina's mother do before. The flat board would be displayed on the dining room table, and the rolling pin would be next to it. They would stand for hours over the dining room table--kneading, rolling, flattening, and evenly cutting the dough strips. Knowing that her grandchildren play sports, practice yoga, and compete in CrossFit, she joked, *see this is my workout.*

Pasqualina sat at the table and winced and scratched her half opened eyes. Her salt and pepper colored hair was dipping past her forehead. The gravity of her build was below her waist. She was nervous to leave the house during this turbulent time since she slipped on a wet leaf in her sixties and broke her ankle. Her legs were not the same even with the knee replacement surgery. She looked her age.

It was so cold the next night.

I called Pasqualina and she asked, *Where are you?* She said this in a powerful tone. *You were supposed to stay by me last night.* I said I would sleep at her house tonight to appease her. She wanted to know what time I would be arriving. She asked what I wanted to eat. I said, "I don't want anything." She replied, *What do mean you don't want anything. So, I'll make you fresh salad.*

I replied, "No." She pressed, *Mushrooms*. I responded, "No." She acquiesced, *Alright*.

We have not had power for eight days. Now a week after the hurricane, they were predicting another storm. This time they said snow. There were still wires down with caution tape around them. Caution tape ran across the width of the street blocking any passage. My neighbor across the street had mounds of material from his house covering the entire circular driveway that lead up to his front porch.

Where do I go now?[11]

I went to Pasqualina's house. She had power and "the power" I thought. I arrived and she was boiling water with little pastina in a dilapidated silver pot. On the stove were about eight chicken cutlet parmesan pieces. The frying pan rested beside it. The pan had a blackened bottom on the exterior, and the pan was probably around for thirty plus years. She had a fully-cooked salmon. She steamed cauliflower. Salad was in the refrigerator. In a pot was the freshly made broth used for chicken soup. Her house was warm. Her son, Pasquale, said "Can you believe how warm it is in here?" She was always trying to conserve the heat. Her son roamed through the half-lit house only to step outside for a cigarette. The pastina was almost ready. She asked who wanted chicken in their soup. Giuseppe came upstairs from his "man cave", and sat and ate with us at the table. We were sitting and eating a bowl of hot pastina. We all added pepper. Pasqualina gave me a piece of quiche and chicken and insisted on giving me more. I did not have the stomach to eat more.

I took a warm shower and wanted to blow dry my hair so I would not fall asleep with wet hair. I took my time. I thanked her immensely. I left to vote.[12] In an updated news blog on CNN on November 1st "President Obama discussed Superstorm Sandy at a campaign rally in Green Bay, Wisconsin, today. 'When disaster strikes, we see America at its best. All the petty differences that consume us in normal times all seem to melt away. There are no Democrats or Republicans during a storm--they're just fellow Americans,' the President said."[13]

After I voted, I arrived at my house, and I was scared. I had a suitcase worth of work in the back seat of my car. I took out a flashlight that was in the car. I used the light as a guide when I walked from the car to the front door and into a dark, empty disarrayed house. I strolled into the silence with my red suitcase; entering complete darkness was unfamiliar and eerie. Sirens from down the street sounded once I was inside. I heard the siren when I tried to write in the afternoon. This afternoon there was a voice coming from the truck with the siren. The voice from the truck echoed there was food.[14] At night it was not the same siren--the night sirens continued to sound and no voices were heard.

I found my way upstairs to my bed. I bundled myself in multiple layers of sweats and wrapped myself in a blanket so I could not move. I thought it funny how involuntary habits were formed. I was conditioned to reach for the light, but there was no light to turn off.

November 8, 2012: Nor-Easter had hit.

We had to evacuate. The prediction for snow became real. I walked out of my office and could not find my car amongst the line of snow covered cars in the parking lot. That day, I went to work early for the supplied power, and after work, I roamed the parking lot with my suitcase. It escaped my mind which car was mine because I was given a temporary rental since my car had been flooded and not drivable. It looked like a winter wonderland. Nothing was plowed. I drove to my aunt's house and stayed with my cousin. My house was too cold. The less time we stayed in my uninhabited house, the colder it became.

This Property is Condemned. No, it was not a Tennessee Williams' play. It was the sign on my neighbor's house. They live five houses down from me and across the street. They now have a mobile home next to their house with holiday lights hanging around it. This was not the only trailer on the block.

Pasqualina continued to cook for us through the second storm and the next three nights. The table was set each night. On the table were forks and knives, glasses, napkins, a tablecloth and a plate of bread or starter. We brought our perishables from our refrigerator and Pasqualina stored it in her garage in a freezer that looked like the size of a coffin. She kept the perishables with her other garden produce that she froze when there was an overabundance.

The stove was running hot. On this night, she made pasta and meatballs and potatoes with manest. These were two classic dishes from her hometown. On Friday, we did not have meat. She made potatoes and eggs, frittata. She had seasoned tilapia, baked mushrooms, eggplant, and salad. Pasquale made and served the coffee. Coffee was made in a large glass pot on the stove. Phyllis washed the dishes.

Today, in New York, rations for gas began. The odd numbered license plates could get gas. I was an odd number. I went in the evening and waited thirty minutes on line in my rent-a-car. I grew anxious approaching the gas pump. No police were in sight. Many people waited with the red gas buckets on a separate line. The station had a cash only policy.[15]

That night, at the table, Pasqualina spoke of rations during the war. Meat was rationed during the war. Pasqualina would be able to get one piece of meat every other Thursday. Her family would split the meat into three pieces. The pieces were not equal in size. There were small, medium, and large slices. Since there were three children in her family, her mother would split it among them. Her mother did not have any. Pasqualina's brother would get the largest piece, then her middle sister would get the next piece, and Pasqualina would get the next piece. She said the reason she would receive the smallest piece was because she was the *smallest* in her family. Because of Pasqualina's position in her family she would eat less.[16] "We may or may not see another storm like Sandy in our lifetimes, but I don't think it's fair to say that we should leave it to our children to prepare for the possibility" said Bloomberg (p. A6).[17]

I stayed with my younger cousin. We turned on the news. In the background in one area on Long Island a sign read "If you loot we will shoot."

Pre-Sandy

It was Pasqualina's 80th birthday a few days before Sandy hit, and a weekend of events were planned. On Friday morning, Phyllis had a breakfast with Pasqualina and her circle of church friends. Matilde was in town and coming to join us for coffee and cake in the early evening. Friday night would be capped off with some wine and a fish dinner with cousins and Pasqualina's sister-in-law, Vincenza.

Phyllis' breakfast had an array of food. It included homemade crepes with fruit, cranberry and blueberry muffins, eggs and sausage in a quiche shape, waffles, whole wheat pancakes, homemade crumb cake, apple cake, tea tarts and croissants. Her friends were lovely and bubbly. They spoke of waist lines and their age. They asked about recipes and tasted new delights. All before the morning rush, they smiled and took photos.

When I came to the party in the afternoon, Matilde was on the sidewalk un-wrapping a cigarette box by the front pail. She wore a blue blazer, fitted dark pants, and low sneakers. Her hair was soft and sophisticated. She wore a red/pinkish hue lipstick. I beeped the horn and she looked up. I pulled in the driveway, and I was warmed with her smile. We hugged tightly.

Pasqualina sat at the head of the table. Her sister-in-law came over, too. Matilde was driven by her sister-in-law as well. We had pizza and demitasse coffee, and Matilde could not sit at the table without going outside every 15 minutes to smoke, just like in Argentina. We took photographs and shared stories. The women spoke in their language--the language of gathering around the table with old friends. This ritual started before their conception. It began with their great grandparents. They left early that evening, and the next morning, before the storm, the tide began to rise.

Matilde was scheduled to leave the following evening. We received word from her daughter through email that she did not leave. They canceled her flight because of Hurricane Sandy. Lucy was not able to change her flight. She told me that Matilde was very "afraid" of storms. We hoped she would make it home.

> Tires pushing puddles
> splatter on the natural canvas
> thrashing branches rancored
> My poor trees
> I cry for the tossed leaves,
> the distressed particles clinging and circling
> waving mercilessly, utterly shaken
> Resisting the uproot
> as sandy's gale gusto rallies
> through park place's hourglass

EPILOGUE

It was a month after Hurricane Sandy. While jogging through my neighborhood, I noticed the cemented sidewalks were still lifted. Branches and stumps were down. The December holidays were approaching and houses on the block had temporary motor homes next to their vacant houses.

    I thought about Airola and my walks and runs through the historic streets that still reflected the damage of 1945. I thought of 'stray dogs' of the past which walked on the same pebbled and dirt roads. During the midday siesta, most of the older population was sleeping, so I either went food shopping or running. When I went running, stray dogs tiptoed by me and I was a dust particle to them--the stray dogs were those who wandered physically in the present and the 'stray dogs' of the past who walked on the same pebble and dirt roads.

I ran by farms. On my run, little bridges were cemented above a small highway that connected to the town, and interrupted the natural fluidity of the provincial area. It appeared like an honest bridging. From the distance, I could see the mountain of Taburno. When I went on these runs, I recalled images. I would remember how people phrased ideas to me. I was called the "American." I thought a female running in Nike shorts and a red tank top with an iPod would look like an American girl. My male cousins asked me to run with them one day. They wore tight spandex and said, "This is how we run here."

In the heat of the day, I continued to run, and I thought of the old women's wise words. As a young woman anywhere, it is advised *to keep your eyes open* (apri gli occhi).

Over the course of the past four years, I have been to many train stations--New York, San Francisco, Philadelphia, Seattle, Washington, D.C., London, Naples, Florence, Rome, Paris and a well of tears fill my eyes when I think about the 'stray dogs' that were picked up and left behind. I try not to blink because the puddle of lessons will become a stream down my cheek. This lens of consciousness was not as obvious at the time, but remains within me, as a transitive presence. The train's function was to pick me up from these places--moments.

These women's lives and being will remain with me and with those who learn of their contributions. And so, we, as humans, grandmothers, mothers, granddaughters, daughters, and mentors become active carriers of their lives.

Pasqualina, Susan, Matilde, and Filomena are each a *custom design*.

RECIPES

*Note: Ingredient amounts are missing for some of the heritage recipes. Consider personal preferences in these instances.

Antipasto Platter

1 fresh homemade mozzarella (sliced)
1 fresh beefsteak tomato (sliced)
1 (6-oz) jar artichokes
Black olives
Green olives
Greek Kalamata olives
Roasted red peppers
½ lb. prosciutto (sliced thin)
½ lb. salami (sliced thin)
1 stick hard dried sausage (sliced)
1 stick soppressata (sliced)
Italian bread sticks

On a large serving platter, arrange fresh mozzarella and tomato slices. Continue to arrange artichokes, roasted red peppers, black, green, Greek olives, hard dried sausage and soppressata. Roll prosciutto and salami slices and arrange on platter. Serve with Italian bread sticks, if desired.

===

Anna's Seafood Salad

Fish made and served on Christmas Eve
1-2 Octopus/Pulpo
1 box of Squid/Calamari (cleaned)
1-2 lbs. Scungilli (cleaned)
1-2 lbs. Shrimp (peeled and deveined)
Fresh squeezed lemon juice (3-6+lemons)
1 can Black olives
1-3 Grated carrots
1-3 Chopped celery

Clean fish. Place whole octopus in pan and steam until it turns pick. Cool and pull off black outer skin. Place the squid, calamari, scungilli, and shrimp individually into pan and steam until it turns color. Cool and chop into bite size pieces. Place in large bowl and mix together. Squeeze in lemon regularly (3-6x). Stir often and keep marinated in refrigerator for a least a day.

***Note: Same fish can be used to make Seafood Mix in a Red Sauce—Make a thick red sauce by allowing to cook for a few hours. Add the raw cleaned and well drained, patted dry pulpo, calamari, scungilli, and shrimp. Add pepper and red hot pepper flakes to taste liking. Allow to simmer for about half hour. Sauce will become thinner—it will make for a great spaghetti and fish sauce. (Great to dip with homemade zeppole) Taste to verify fish is cooked and enough spices before serving.

===

Baked Clams alla Nannina

3-5 dozen medium to large size raw clams (opened, cleaned, and chopped)
1 tsp. fresh parsley (chopped)
2-3 garlic cloves (minced)
1/3—1/4 cup olive oil

Fresh clam juice
Black pepper
Freshly grated bread crumbs (or seasoned bread crumbs)
Cleaned clam shells—brush with olive oil

Open raw clams over a wide bowl to catch dripping clam juice and clear black from the clam. Chop clams in a separate bowl. Add chopped fresh parsley, garlic, olive oil, reserved claim juice, black pepper and enough bread crumbs to bind the mixture. Scoop by tablespoon onto cleaned oil brushed clam shell. Bake in preheated oven at 360° for 30 minutes. Broil top of clams for 5 minutes or until lightly browned.

===

Bruschetta

1 loaf of very thin French bread (sliced about ¼ inch)
Seasoned olive oil with black pepper and oregano
1 fresh tomato (chopped)
1 onion (chopped)
2-3 garlic cloves (minced)
Fresh basil (chopped)
Black pepper
Oregano

Preheat oven at 350°. In bowl, combine the tomato, onion, garlic, basil, black pepper, and oregano. Set aside. Coat baking sheet with olive oil. Line baking sheet with sliced bread. Brush bread slices with seasoned olive oil. Place in oven and slightly brown bread slices on each side. Using teaspoon, top bread slices with seasoned tomato mixture. Return to oven and allow tomato mixture to warm.

===

Bow Tie Pasta with Broccoli Rabe

1 box Rotini or bow tie pasta
1 lb. fresh broccoli rabe
2 tbsp. extra virgin olive oil
2 garlic cloves (minced)
Black pepper
Oregano
Extra virgin olive oil
Crushed red hot pepper (optional)

    Break leaves from broccoli rabe bunch and remove undesired portion. Place in large bowl and add water. Wash, rinse, and drain broccoli rabe. Pat dry with paper towel. In a large frying pan, add olive oil and light brown garlic and add broccoli rabe. Cover with lid and cook at low flame for about 15 minutes or until desired tenderness, stirring gently occasionally. Turn off flame. Once cooled, chop broccoli rabe and set aside. Cook pasta al dente or desired taste. Drain and place in large bowl. Pour olive oil and sprinkle with pepper, oregano, crushed red pepper, and toss with broccoli rabe.

***Note: Any favorite vegetable may be used in place of broccoli rabe.

===

Beef Bracciole

2-lb. London Broil or flank steak or desired beef strip
2-3 garlic cloves (minced)
Fresh parsley (chopped)
Parmesan cheese
Black pepper
Oregano
Food wrapping white string
¼ cup white or red wine

Slice London Broil top side, long lengthwise to make wide strips. Lay out slices on wax paper. Sprinkle each slice with black pepper, oregano, cheese parsley, and garlic. Roll up tightly from smaller to wider end. With food string, wrap around tightly and knot. Braise rolled up pieces in frying pan with 2-3 tablespoons of olive oil, browning on each side. Just before removing from frying pan, add wine and simmer for 1-2 minutes. Remove from pan and drain. When ready, allow to cook in pot of thick cooking tomato sauce for about 1 hour.

===

Chicken Cacciatore

1 whole chicken (cut up) or mixed parts
2-3 tbsp. olive oil
1 small onion (chopped)
1-2 garlic cloves (minced)
½ cup flour
Black pepper
½ cup white wine
½ cup low sodium chicken broth
1-2 cups whole tomatoes (crushed)
Fresh basil
Black pepper
Crush red pepper
Oregano

Place cut up chicken in salted cold water. Remove any excess fat. Rinse in fresh water, drain, and pat dry. In large, wide-based frying pan, pour olive oil and sauté onion and garlic until tender. In flat dish, add flower and black pepper. Coat chicken lightly in seasoned flour and brown on all sides in heated oil with onion and garlic. Pour white wine, chicken broth, and whole crushed tomatoes. Allow to simmer for 10 minutes. Sprinkle with black pepper, crush red pepper, oregano, and basil. Transfer into Pyrex or Corningware baking dish and cook in preheated over at 350° for 1 ½ hours or more.

***Note: Peeled, cubed potatoes may be added to chicken and tomatoes for the last 45 minutes for a chicken and potato dish.

===

Italian Wedding Soup

2-3 lbs. escarole
2-3 tbsp. olive oil
1-2 garlic cloves (minced)
1-2 cans (12 oz.) low sodium beef broth
Black pepper
Oregano
Meatballs (made small) (See recipe below) or Italian sausage (cooked and cubed)

Tear escarole leaves into pieces. Soak in water. Wash, rinse, and drain. In a large cooking pot, add water and bring to a boil. Add washed escarole leaves to boiling water; cook for 2-3 minutes. Remove escarole leaves, drain and chop into bite size pieces. Save escarole water. Set aside both chopped escarole and water. In a medium-size pot, pour oil and sauté garlic cloves. Do not burn. Add drained escarole and sauté for 1-2 minutes. Pour in beef broth. For each can of broth, add saved escarole water. Sprinkle with black pepper and oregano. Simmer for 10 minutes. Add cooked small meatballs (or sausage) and simmer for about 5-7 minutes. Serve.

===

Homemade Chicken Soup

1 small whole chicken or fowl
1 small onion (sliced lengthwise)
3-4 carrots (skinned and cut in thirds)
3-4 celery stalks (skinned and cut in thirds)
1 whole canned or homemade jarred tomatoes
Whole black peppercorns
Black pepper
Oregano
Fresh dill (chopped)

    In a large pot, place whole chicken in cold salted water. Be sure to clean interior. Let chicken set in salted water for about ½ hour. Scrub and rinse chicken. In large pot, fill ¾ of the pot with water. Place clean whole chicken in pot. Add onions, carrots, celery, tomatoes, peppercorns, black pepper, oregano, and chopped dill. Cook covered over high flame until it comes to a boil. Simmer at low heat for 2-3 hours. Let cool and place in refrigerator overnight. Skim fat from top, if any. Drain liquid. Cook tortellini or small Ditalini pasta or any small-sized desired pasta, as directed. Drain pasta. Add homemade chicken broth. Add shredded chicken meat and/or cooked carrots to pasta and broth, if desired.

===

Homemade Meatballs

1 ½ - 2 lbs. ground round beef chopped meat (raw) (lean--90%)
½ - 1 lb. ground pork meat (raw) **or** 6 links of sausage (removed from casing)
3-4 eggs (beaten)
Italian stale bread
Fresh parsley (chopped)
2 garlic cloves (minced)
Parmesan cheese

Black pepper
Oregano

Cook tomato sauce (see recipe below) for at least 1 hour. Soak the stale Italian bread in warm water until softened. Remove from water and squeeze excess water. In a large bowl, combine the beef and pork meats. Add beaten eggs, shredded squeezed bread, parsley, garlic, Parmesan cheese, black pepper, and oregano. Mix well using hands. Roll meat mixture in the shape of a ball to desired size. Place on lightly greased baking sheet and bake at 375° for 7-10 minutes on one side. Turn meatballs over and bake for another 5-7 minutes or until golden on outer sides. You need not cook meatballs as they will cook in the tomato sauce. Remove excess on sides of meatballs. Gently drop into thick cooking tomato sauce. Cook at low heat for about 1 hour. Serve with pasta or great in a hero roll or Italian bread.

*****Note**: Light and dark chopped turkey meat can be substituted for turkey balls.

==

Lasagna

1-2 lbs. chopped meat (lean) browned
2 tbsp. olive oil
Cooked tomato sauce
1 box Barilla or San Giorgio Lasagna
2 lb. can part-skim ricotta cheese
1 (8-oz.) mozzarella part-skim cheese (cubed)
2 eggs (beaten)
1 tbsp. chopped parsley
Black pepper
Parmesan cheese
Cooked tomato sauce

Cook a pot of tomato sauce (see recipe below). In frying pan, heat 2 tablespoons of olive oil and brown chop meat. Drain chop meat in colander. After tomato sauce cooks for 1 hour, add browned, drained chop meat. Cook for another 1 hour. Prepare ricotta mixture by blending ricotta cheese, eggs, parsley, and black pepper. Set aside until ready to use. Cube mozzarella cheese and set aside until ready to use. In a large pot, bring water to boil. Add salt to water. Gently place lasagna pasta in salted boiling water and cook for 3-5 minutes. Do not fully cook as lasagna cooks again in oven. Gently drain and quickly layout on waxed paper so lasagna remains straight. In rectangular glass baking dish, coat bottom of dish with tomato sauce. Line first layer of lasagna. Cut and shape lasagna to coat entire bottom of dish. Spread with ricotta/egg mixture, then chop meat tomato sauce, followed by mozzarella cheese and sprinkle with parmesan cheese. Continue this process until pan is filled. Preheat oven at 350°. Bake lasagna for 15 minutes uncovered and then covered with aluminum foil for 15 more minutes for a total of ½ hour cooking time. Let it set covered for 15-30 minutes in oven. Remove from oven and serve.

*****Note**: For vegetable lasagna, replace meat with fresh cauliflower (flowerets), fresh broccoli (flowerets) diced red pepper, diced green pepper, and can of peas. Cook fresh cauliflower and broccoli in tomato sauce for about 15 minutes. Red and green peppers and pea need not cook in sauce—merely add over ricotta mixture with vegetable tomato sauce.

*****Note**: Any favorite vegetable may be used, i.e. artichoke hearts, spinach, etc.

===

Potato & Egg Frittata

3-4 all-purpose potatoes (peeled & cubed)
3-4 tbsp. vegetable oil
4 eggs (beaten)

Black pepper
Parmesan cheese

    Heat vegetable oil in frying pan. Brown potatoes in heated oil. Remove potatoes and drain. Beat eggs, pepper, and cheese in large bowl. Mix potatoes into egg mixture. Stir until well blended. Return to heated pan and cook at medium heat. Place flat dish that fits over frying pan and flip over and cook other side.

===

Sausage & Peppers

6 links of Italian sausage or one medium sized thin round link
2 red bell peppers (sliced)
2 green bell peppers (sliced)
1 large onion (sliced thin)
Extra virgin olive oil
Black pepper

    Broil or grill sausage, turning until all sides are golden brown. Set aside. Place peppers and onion on baking sheet. Coat with olive oil and black pepper. Broil or grill peppers and onions, and turning until all sides are roasted and tender. Cut sausage until ½-inch slices. Mix with peppers and onions. Combine all ingredients

*****Note**: Add cooked tomato sauce over sausage and peppers, if desired. Makes great sausage, peppers, and onion heroes.

===

Spaghetti with Clam Sauce

3-4 doz. small clams (scrubbed clean on outer shell)
3 tbsp. extra virgin oil
2 garlic cloves (minced)
Fresh parsley (chopped)
Black pepper
Crushed red hot pepper
1 box thin spaghetti or linguini

Scrub clean outer shell of clams. Pat dry. Set aside. In large pot, pour olive oil and light brown garlic. Add black pepper. Gently place clams in pot and cover. Keep at medium to high heat until all clams open. Do not remove lid. Once clam shells open, sprinkle with parsley. Set aside. Cook spaghetti al dente or desired texture. Drain pasta. Mix with clam juice and top with clams.

===

Stuffed Baked Shells

1 box pasta shells
1 (15 oz.) can part-skim ricotta cheese
1 egg (beaten)
1 (8-oz.) mozzarella part-skim cheese (shredded)
Fresh parsley (chopped)
Parmesan cheese
Black pepper
Oregano
Tomato Sauce

Cook a pot of homemade tomato sauce. (See recipe) In a medium mixing bowl, prepare ricotta mix by blending with electric mixer the ricotta cheese, shredded mozzarella, egg, parsley, Parmesan cheese, black pepper, and oregano. Set aside in refrigerator until ready to use. In a large pot, bring water to boil. Add salt to taste. Gently place pasta shells in salted water and cook for 3-5 minutes. Do not fully cook as shells will cook again in oven. Gently drain and cool enough to handle. Fill each shell with enough cheese mixture to close shell. Avoid overstuffing. In a rectangular glass baking dish, coat bottom of dish with tomato sauce. Place stuffed ricotta shells next to each other until dish is filled. Scoop homemade tomato over stuffed shells. Sprinkle additional mozzarella cheese and Parmesan cheese. Preheat oven at 350°. Bake shells for 15 minutes uncovered and then covered with aluminum foil for 10-15 minutes for a total of a ½ hour cooking time. Allow pasta shells to set covered for about ½ hour in oven. Remove from oven and serve.

*****Note**: For meat filling—In frying pan, heat 2 tablespoons of olive oil and cook lean chopped meat just until brown. Drain chopped meat using colander. Add cooked lean chopped meat to the ricotta filling.

==

Tomato Sauce (Homemade)

During the month of August, once the home-grown tomatoes (Roma—oblong shaped) are ripe, the tomatoes are picked and laid to ripen until ready to bottle or jar. This is a production process and stored throughout the year.

1 bottled or jarred preserved homemade tomato sauce
1 jar preserved whole peeled tomatoes (diced)
2-3 tbsp. olive oil
1 garlic clove (chopped)

In a medium-sized sauce pan, pour olive oil and garlic. Allow garlic to brown lightly. Do not burn. Add jar of preserved diced peeled tomatoes and cook uncovered at medium to low heat for 20-30 minutes. Add bottle of tomato sauce and allow to come to a boil. Simmer at low heat for a least an hour. The longer the sauce simmers, the better.

*****Note**: For **Homemade Tomato Meat Sauce**—In frying pan, add olive oil. Once olive oil is heated, add about 1-pound lean ground chopped meat and brown. Drain chopped meat in colander to allow excess oil to drip. Add drained chop meat and simmer for 30-45 minutes. The longer the sauce cooks, the better.

*****Note**: For **Homemade Italian Sunday Meat Sauce**—3-6 fresh broiled Italian sausage links, 2-3 braised bracciole, 3-4 braised beef short ribs, 3-4 braised pork ribs, 3-4 braised lamb bones, and homemade meatballs (See recipe). Use a very large pot to start cooking the tomato sauce. Once the plain homemade tomato sauce cooks for 1-1/2 hours, place the braised rib and bone meats first and simmer for about 1-1/2 hours, then sausage links and meatballs for another hour. Allow to simmer for total of 2-3 hours. The longer it simmers, the tastier. Remove meats and place in serving platter. Use sauce to coat and cover cooked pasta. Serve pasta with meats. Sunday Meat Sauce may be cooked a day before. Refrigerate overnight and then skim any fat from the top.

*****Note**: Braised pig's feet, knuckles, and/or pork skin bracciole may be added to pot of meat sauce.

==

Veal Prosciutto & Mozzarella Roll Ups

1-2 lbs. lean Italian veal cutlets (sliced thin & long)
2-3 tbsp. olive oil
½ tbsp. butter or margarine
1 garlic clove (minced)
Flour
Black pepper
Oregano
1 stick butter
1 tsp. fresh parsley (chopped)
2-3 garlic cloves (minced)

Black pepper
¼ lb. prosciutto (sliced thin)
(4 oz.) part-skim mozzarella cheese (sliced thin)

In frying pan, pour oil, butter, and garlic. Over medium flame, allow garlic to slightly turn brown. Coat veal cutlets lightly in seasoned flour mixture (pepper and oregano). Sauté floured veal cutlets on each side for 2-3 minutes or until brown. Remove from pan and drain any excess oil. Lay cooled veal cutlets on waxed paper. Place a layer of thinly sliced mozzarella cheese and prosciutto and roll, sticking with toothpicks to hold securely. Place seam side down into baking cookware. Melt butter or margarine, chopped parsley, garlic, and black pepper in small frying pan, just until it comes to a slight boil. Do not burn garlic. Pour butter mixture over rolled veal cutlets. Bake at 350° for 20 minutes. Turn off oven and let set covered with aluminum foil for 5-10 minutes.

==

Tripe

1-2 pkgs. Tripe
Cooked tomato sauce
Red hot crushed pepper
Black pepper
Oregano

Cook tomato sauce (See recipe). Bring water to boil in large pot. Cook tripe at medium heat for 10-15 minutes. Drain and rinse tripe. Remove any excess fat. Cut into bite size morsels. Add tripe to cooked tomato sauce. Add red hot crushed pepper, black pepper, and oregano. Cook the tripe for about 1-2 hours or until tender.

==

Turkey Stuffing

2-3 pkgs. turkey and/or chicken gizzards
2 tbsp. extra virgin olive oil
½ Italian round stale bread
2-3 eggs (beaten)
½ cup low sodium chicken or turkey broth
2 garlic cloves (minced)
Fresh parsley (chopped)
Parmesan cheese
Black pepper

In a medium saucepan, bring gizzards to boil for 3-5 minutes. Drain and rinse. Chop gizzards into very small pieces. In a frying pan, pour olive oil. Braise gizzards. Stir continuously and allow to cook for 20-30 minutes. Drain and set aside. Soak stale bread in warm water just until bread is moist and squeeze excess water. In a large mixing bowl, shred the moistened bread and combined with gizzards, eggs, garlic cloves, fresh parsley, black pepper, cheese, and enough broth to allow for binding. Stuffing can be inserted into turkey and/or shaped in a mound and placed in a greased baking dish pan. Cook in preheated oven at 350° for 45-60 minutes or until golden on top. Do not overcook.

===

Vegetable Soup

1 small onion (chopped)
2 garlic cloves (minced)
2 tbsp. olive oil
2 strips bacon (chopped) (optional)
1 head fresh broccoli (cut into small flowerets)
1 head fresh cauliflower (cut into small flowerets)
2-3 fresh carrots (cubed)
2-3 celery stalks (cubed)

1 fresh zucchini (cubed)
1 (10 oz.) can peas (drained)
2-3 cups vegetable broth
Black pepper
Oregano

In a large pot, pour the olive oil, sauté the onions and garlic until tender. Add the bacon, if desired, and cook until browned. Add one vegetable at a time to allow each to cook 5 minutes before adding the next. Begin with vegetable that takes the longest to cook—cauliflower, carrots, broccoli, zucchini, and peas. Add the vegetable broth to fill ¾ of the pot. Season with black pepper and oregano. Simmer for about 15 minutes.

***Note: Add Ditalini pasta to make Minestrone Soup. Lentils can also be added to vegetables. Cook lentils according to package.

===

Artichoke and Sausage Quiche

1 (12-oz,) frozen pie crust (thawed)
Fresh artichoke hearts -or- 1 (9-oz.) frozen artichoke hearts (thawed)
1 (8-oz) mozzarella cheese (cubed)
6-8 cooked Italian sausage links (diced)
4-5 eggs (beaten)
Pepper
Parmesan cheese

Preheat oven to 350°. Combine artichoke hearts, sausage, and mozzarella cheese in large bowl. Stir in eggs, pepper, and cheese. Mix well. Pour into pie shell. Bake for 1 hour or until firm. Turn off oven and let set for ½ hour. Remove from oven and serve.

===

Broccoli and Cheddar Quiche

1 (12-oz.) frozen pie crust (thawed)
Fresh broccoli flowerets –or-- 1 (9-oz.) frozen broccoli (thawed & drained)
1 (8-oz.) cheddar cheese (cubed)
4 eggs (beaten)
Pepper
Parmesan cheese

Preheat oven to 350°. Combine broccoli and cheddar cheese in large bowl. Stir in eggs, cheese, and pepper. Mix well. Pour into pie shell. Bake for approximately 45 minutes or until firm. Turn off oven and let set for about 15 minutes. Remove from oven and serve.

==

Spinach Quiche

Oven Temperature: 350°

Ingredients

Frozen pie crust (thawed)
Package of fresh spinach. (1 package frozen spinach (thawed) and also be used)
3-4 beaten eggs
Parmesan cheese
Black pepper
Diced mozzarella cubes

Preheat oven to 350°. Squeeze excess water from frozen spinach. Place in mixing bowl. Add beaten eggs, parmesan cheese, and black pepper. Stir in diced mozzarella cubes. Top with shredded mozzarella.

Bake for half hour or until solidified. Turn off oven and let set for about 15 minutes.

**Note: Spinach and mozzarella can be substituted with broccoli and cheddar cheese.

***Note: Mushrooms can also be added.

===

Eggplant Rollatini

Oven Temperature: 350°

Ingredients

1-2 oblong medium-size eggplants
2-3 eggs
parmesan cheese
black pepper
chopped parsley
seasoned bread crumbs
Ricotta
Mozzarella (grated or thinly sliced)
Pepper

Peel and slice eggplants lengthwise. Soak in salted water. Drain and place heavy item over colander to squeeze out excess water. In large enough deep bowl, beat eggs, cheese, pepper and chopped parsley. On a flat plate, place bread crumbs. Dip eggplant in egg batter and then in bread crumbs. Fry in vegetable oil, brown on each side, and drain on paper towels. Cool. Arrange eggplant on wax paper. Sprinkle with black pepper, parmesan cheese, grated mozzarella and ½ tsp ricotta. Roll each eggplant. Placing the edge side down, arrange on tomato sauce coated baking pan. Top with tomato sauce. Top with thin sliced or grated mozzarella. Bake in preheated oven at 350° for 15-20 minutes. Turn off the oven and let it set for about 10-15 minutes covered with aluminum foil.

Risotto

1 cup Arborio risotto rice
2-3 tbsp. olive oil
1 small onion (chopped)
1 garlic clove (minced)
Black pepper
Oregano
1 can low sodium beef broth
Fresh parsley (chopped)
¼ cup white wine
1 (10-oz.) can peas (drained), if desired
1 (6-oz.) can mushroom (stemmed & drained), if desired

In a medium to large size pot, pour olive oil and sauté onions and garlic until tender. Sprinkle with black pepper and oregano. Stir in rice until brown for 1-2 minutes. At low heat, gradually add beef broth (1/4 cup at a time) until broth evaporates each time. Repeat process until broth can is empty. This will take about 20-30 minutes. If additional liquid is needed, add water. Just before the last liquid evaporation, add ¼ cup white wine, fresh parsley, and drained peas and/or mushrooms.

***Note: Lobster or shrimp pieces may be added to the end of the cooking process and cooked for 5 minutes to make for a seafood risotto.

===

String Bean, Red Pepper, Cauliflower Blend

½ lb. fresh string beans
2 red bell peppers
2 small cauliflower
¼ cup white vinegar
Black pepper

Oregano
Garlic (chopped)

Snap tips, wash, and drain string beans. Place in boiling water for 5-7 minutes. Add white vinegar for last two minutes of cooking. Drain and cool. Break cauliflower into small flowerets. Wash, rinse, and drain. Place in pot with little water and allow to steam for 8-10 minutes. Add white vinegar for last two minutes of cooking. Drain and cool. Wash and wipe red bell peppers. Cut length wise. Place coated (olive oil) baking sheet, sprinkle with pepper, and broil until slightly roasted all around. Remove from oven and cool. Lay out red, green, and white vegetables on a large serving platter. Sprinkle with pepper, oregano, and chopped garlic, if desired.

==

Stuffed Red Peppers Vinaigrette

Typical vegetable served with fish on Christmas Eve

6-8 small whole red rounded peppers (placed in white vinegar)
1-2 portions of stale Italian round bread (softened in warm water and excess water squeezed)
1 can (10-oz.) black olives (chopped)
Walnuts (chopped)
Raisins
Pignoli nuts
2-3 anchovies (chopped)
Black pepper
Oregano

Small whole red peppers should be pickled in white vinegar for a few days/weeks and kept in refrigerator. When ready to stuff, drain peppers well. In a bowl, allow stale Italian bread to soak in warm water, but not too long. Drain and squeeze excess water. In large bowl, shred bread into small pieces, add chopped nuts, raisins, pignoli nuts, anchovies, black pepper, and oregano. Mix well. Stuff vinaigrette red peppers. In frying pan, coat bottom with olive oil. Brown bread stuffing side first until crusted and continue to brown on all sides. Place in baking pan, drizzle with olive oil, and bake for 20-30 minutes at 325°.

===

Cannoli Filling

1 (15 oz.) **WHOLE** ricotta cheese (drained)
2 tsp. sugar
2 tsps. Confectioners sugar
2-3 tsp. anisette liquor
1 cup mini semi-sweet chocolate chips

Drain ricotta cheese. In medium mixing bowl, mix ricotta with electric mixer at low speed for about 2 minutes. Gradually add sugar and Confectioners sugar. Taste for additional sugar, if desired. Continue to mix at low to medium speed. Stir in anisette liquor. Note consistency. Avoid making it too liquid. Cream should have firm consistency. Fold in chocolate chips and refrigerate overnight. Fill any cake, cannoli shells, cream puff, etc.

===

Easter—La Pizza Piena—The Full Pie
The Rich Man's Pie/The Money Pie
Pizza Rustica

Make on Good Friday

1 (2 lb.) or (3 lb.) can ricotta
1-1 ½ dozen eggs

1-1 ½ lb. prosciutto (cubed)
1-2 links dry hard sausage (cubed)
1 16 oz. mozzarella (cubed)
1 basket fresh mozzarella (cubed)
pie crusts (either frozen or homemade)

Prepare large rectangular corningware with pie crust. Cube the prosciutto, hard sausage, and mozzarella—set aside. In large pot, mix ricotta and eggs. Stir in the cubed prosciutto, hard sausage and mozzarella. Pour mixed batter into prepared pie crust corningware. Cube the fresh mozzarella and place on top of batter.

Cook pies in preheated over at 350° for 1-1 ½ hour or until golden on top. Let set in oven. Remove from oven and allow to cool on counter. Cover and refrigerate overnight.

***Note**: Do not add any salt or pepper as prosciutto and sausage will allow for salt. You may want to add additional ricotta and/or eggs to absorb the salted flavor.

==

Easter—Sweet Pie—Pizza Dolce

Make on Good Friday for Easter
Can also be made for Palm Sunday

Preheat oven to 350°

1 (2 lb.) can **whole** ricotta
½ cup sugar
8-10 large eggs
1 tablespoon anisette
1 tablespoon rum
1 tablespoon vanilla

1 package of graham cracker crust
½ stick of softened butter/margarine

Crumble graham cracker crust in blender until fine. Put crumbled graham crackers in bowl and mix with softened butter or margarine. Prepare corningware with crumbled graham cracker crust. Pat firmly in corningware and bake crumbs for 5-10 minutes. Let cool. Pour ricotta in large bowl and begin mixing for about 1-2 minutes. Gradually pour in sugar. Beat eggs, one at a time and then finish mixing at high speed. Stir in anisette, rum and vanilla.

Pour into prepared corningware. After ½ hour baking time, you may wish to gently moisten top of pie with some anisette or rum. Bake for 1-1 1/2 hours or until firm. Let it set in oven for a while and then remove and let cool on counter. Cover and refrigerate overnight.

===

Easter Bread

2 packages dry yeast
½ cup warm water
1 cup milk
½ cup sugar
1 stick sweet butter
½ stick salted butter
¼ teaspoon anise seed
2 eggs
5 cups flour
1 beaten egg yolk
Sesame seeds

Dissolve 2 packages of dry yeast into ½ cup warm water. Blend well for about 2 minutes. In a large pot, heat milk, sugar, and butters. Let cool to lukewarm. Add the yeast mixture to the pot. Add 2 cups of flour and mix.

Beat eggs and add to mixture. Add 3 more cups of flour. Mix well. Knead a few minutes. Cover and let rise for a few hours.

Put on board and knead a few minutes. Make roll and braid into loaves. Place on greased pan. Cover and let rise for 4 hours. Coat top with beaten egg yolk and sprinkle with sesame seeds. Bake at 325°—350° for about ½ hour.

===

Balome (High One)
Easter Panettone

5 cups flour
½ cup sugar
¼ teaspoon salt
1 package dry yeast (dissolved in about 4 oz. of water)
1 stick of butter
1 tablespoon Crisco
7 eggs (room temperature)
1 teaspoon vanilla
1 teaspoon lemon
1 teaspoon orange
1 grated lemon
1 grated orange

Mix dry ingredients together. Combine butter and Crisco into dry ingredients. Blend well the eggs, vanilla, lemon, orange, and grated lemon and orange. In a large bowl, mix well into dry ingredients. Mixing with electronic machine is better. Transfer into well- greased tube pan. Cover with lid, secure with warm covering. Let it rise for hours. Gently place onto baking sheet and bake in preheated oven of 350° for about 1 hour or until top browns and toothpick comes out clean. Remove from oven and cool. Once cooled, whisk 1 egg white and brush over bread. Drizzle with sprinkles.

Zeppoles

5 cups of flour
1 tbsp. salt
One package dry active yeast
1/2-1 cup warm water

In a large pot, dissolve yeast and enough water, and mix into flour and salt until elastic like. Cover with lid and place dish cloth or warm covering over the pot. Let rise for half a day or so. By teaspoon or handful, shape and drop into preheated deep fryer. If cooking over stove, be sure there is enough preheated vegetable oil to cover zeppole. Cook at high to medium heat. Be sure to allow inside to cook. Drain on paper towel. Sprinkle with confectioners sugar, if desired.

Cheesecake

Oven Temperature: 350°

2 prepared Keebler Ready Made Graham Cracker pie crusts
1 package (8 oz.) cream cheese (softened)
½ cup sugar
3 eggs (room temperature)
1 tsp. vanilla
1 ½ container of sour cream

Preheat oven to 350°. Mix cream cheese and sugar in large bowl at medium speed. Add eggs one at a time. Beat thoroughly. Add sour cream and vanilla. Pour batter evenly into each pie crust.

Bake for half hour. Turn off oven and let set for another half hour. Place on counter for another half hour and refrigerate.

***Note**: Cheesecake can be topped with fruit—cherry, strawberry, blueberry, pineapple, fresh fruit

***Note**: By reducing the sour cream, add 1 cup of pumpkin puree for pumpkin cheesecake

***Note**: By reducing the sour cream, add ½ cup whipped eggnog and ½ cup of whipped heavy cream for eggnog cheesecake.

***Note**:   Pour mixture into one pie shell.

With remaining mixture, stir in ½ cup of melted semi-sweet chocolate for a chocolate cheesecake. You will then have one plain cheesecake and one chocolate cheesecake.

===

Tiramisu

5 eggs
1 container (16 oz.) mascarpone cheese
5 tablespoons sugar
1 package Savoiardi cookies (lady fingers)
1 pot of espresso coffee (cold)
Cinnamon and grated chocolate or mini chocolate chips
Brandy or cognac

Separate egg yolks and whites. In a bowl, mix egg yolks, sugar, and cheese.
Beat the egg whites in small bowl until firm and forms peaks. Fold egg whites into yolk mixture. In a glass Pyrex oblong pan, spread cream mixture first. Then place dipped lady finger cookies into cold coffee (do it quickly

so cookie will not be too moist). Line cookie on cream mixture. Sprinkle with cinnamon and brandy. Repeat with additional layers of lady fingers and cream mixture. Decorate with cinnamon and grated chocolate. Cover and refrigerate overnight.

***Note**: This recipe may make two servings trays.

Consider reducing the ingredients in half.

==

Cream Puffs

Preheat oven to 350° In a saucepan, bring to boil

1 cup of water
1 stick of butter
¼ teaspoon of salt
Once boiled, reduce heat and add
1 cup of flour
Stir over low heat continuously until batter moves away from side of the pan (about 5 minutes)
Let the flour mixture cool
Stir one egg at a time
4 eggs in total (**ROOM TEMPERATURE**)
Stir vigorously and with much energy

Add 1 teaspoon of baking powder. Continue to stir until mixed well.
By teaspoon or tablespoon (depending on desired size) drop on very slightly greased cookie sheet. Bake for 25-30 minutes until puffs rise and are golden on top. Try not to open oven door or disturb baking process. Turn off oven and let it stay in oven for another 10 minutes. Then remove from the oven and cool.

Cream Filling:

In medium size saucepan, add
6 egg yolks and stir
½ cup of sugar and stir
6 tablespoons of flour and stir
Stir in about 1 ¾ cups of whole milk (the equivalent of 1 and ½ medium size glass) *
Be sure mixture is dissolved even if you need to squeeze mixture with hand
*Use chocolate milk if you wish to have chocolate filling.

Cook over medium to low heat, stirring one way, continuously until it begins to bubble. Let cool on counter and then in refrigerator overnight. Cut puffs in half and fill with cream or place cream into pastry bag and squeeze into puff. Fill puffs and sprinkle with confectioners sugar.

===

Recipe for Anisette Cookies (Ingenettes)
Grandma's Signature Cookie

Preheat the oven to 350°. In a bowl, combine the following:
3 – 3 ½ cups of flour (Start with 3 cups)
3 – 3 ½ teaspoons of baking powder
½ teaspoon of salt
Place this on a kneading board in the form of a fountain—bringing flour to the sides. In a bowl, mix the following:
3 eggs (**Room Temperature**)
¾ cup of orange juice
½ cup of Wesson vegetable oil
1 teaspoon of vanilla
1 teaspoon of anisette
½ cup of sugar

Slowly pour the liquid ingredients in the middle of the flour, stirring with your hand or a wooden spoon until the two are blended to form a kneading base. Knead for about 5-10 minutes. Set in the corner of the board and cut pieces to form a rolled out long piece that can be formed as a spiral. Set on an ungreased cookie baking pan. Cook for 30 minutes or until golden brown. Let cool.

Frosting—

Stir in deep bowl:
Confectioners sugar
1-2 tablespoons of milk
1 tablespoon of anisette
Mixture should not be too liquidity. Let cool on waxed paper.

===

Holiday Cutout Cookies (Zia Pasqualina's Recipe)

Oven Temperature: 350 °

Ingredients
4 cups flour
2 sticks butter (softened)
4 tsp baking powder
4 eggs
½ cup sugar
1 tsp brandy
1 tsp lemon
1 tsp rum
1 tsp vanilla

Preheat oven to 350°. In large bowl, blend flour and butter until crinkled in texture.

Add the 4 tsp of baking powder. In a separate bowl, mix eggs, sugar, brandy, lemon, rum and vanilla. Pour liquid mixture into flour mixture and gradually stir with spoon until form takes place. Transfer the blended flour mixture on a kneading board. Knead texture for about 5 minutes, until there is an elasticity to the mixture. Additional flour may be added, if needed. Cut dough into sections. Add chocolate chips in one section; raisins to another section, or chopped nuts to another, etc. Use cookie roller to spread out dough as thin as possible. Use cookie cutters and top with sprinkles. Bake for 10-15 minutes

===

Tea Tarts

Oven Temperature: 350 °

Ingredients
1 cup flour
¼ lb. butter (softened)
3 oz. cream cheese (softened)

Mix cream cheese and butter at low speed. Add flour a little at a time until blended.

Roll dough into 24 pieces. Shape each piece into mini muffin pan. Preheat oven to 350°.

Filling:
½ cup brown sugar
1 cup chopped walnuts
1 egg
3 tsp vanilla

Add brown sugar to walnuts. Blend vanilla and egg. Mix well. By teaspoon, drop into lined muffin pan. Bake for 25-30 minutes.

IDIOMATIC EXPRESSIONS FROM AIROLA

The language from the women's region will die with them. Listed are more idiomatic expressions spoken by the women in their native language.

- Quando si mangia si cobatte con la morte

When you eat, you're fighting with death

- L'altezza 'e mezza bellezza

Tallness is half your beauty

- Ai paura che il culo si mangia la camicia

You are afraid that the behind will eat the night gown

- La capa 'e chiamato cocozza

Your head is called a pumpkin (It's empty; it has no taste)

- Fa bene e scrodati. Fa male e pensaci.

Do good and forget about it. Do bad and think about it.

- Non hai bisogno di un indovino per vedere il futuro

You don't need a fortune teller to view the future

- Che non succedo in un anno, succedo in un ora

What doesn't happen in a year, can happen in an hour

ENDNOTES

1. Susan (her adopted American name) referred to her good friend as Anna in all of her conversations.
2. (Personal Communication Linda Longmire, 2011)
3. Rifkin, (2004). Rifkin, J. (2004). *The European dream: how Europe's vision of the future is quietly eclipsing the American dream.* Cambridge, UK: Polity Press.
4. Particular phrases like "backyard" make me think of the person who had said it, my grandfather. The story behind the word, and the pronunciation of the word.
5. Other books on her mantle were: *Professional baking, Vegetarian Feasts, After Dinner drinks, The Complete Book of Desserts, Books on vitamins and minerals, Uprisings: the Whole Grain Baker's Book, Modern Encyclopedia of Herbs, Vibrant Health, Herbs on your Health, Probiotics Revolution* by: Gary Huffnagie; *Food as Medicine* by: Dharma Singh Khalsa
6. *Italian Notebook.* (2012 May 2010). San Pasquale. Retrieved from http://www.italiannotebook.com/events/san-pasquale/. Brief biography on Padre Pio:

    "Padre Pio was born on March 25, 1887 and was born in the Province of Benevento. Padre Pio is a modern day saint to the province of Benevento. We visited his shrine in the town of San Giovanni Rotondo. San Pasquale is the patron saint of fertility, wealth, and abundance. The citizens of Airola are devoted to him as he is considered the protector of women and animals."
7. *An Encyclopedia Britannica: Merriam Webster.* (2013). Faith. Retrieved from http://www.merriam-webster.com/dictionary/faith.
8. Swami T. (2009, May 27). On Faith and Reason. *Harmonist.* Retrieved from http://harmonist.us/2009/05/on-faith-and-reason/
9. *The Canterbury Tales Project.* University of Birmingham. Retrieval date 20 Jan 2013. Retrieved from http://www.canterburytalesproject.org/. "A pilgrimage is a journey or search of moral spiritual significance. Typically, it is a journey to a shrine or other location of importance to a person's beliefs and faith, although sometimes it can be a metaphorical journey in to someone's own

beliefs." This word also conjures up the context of Canterbury's Tale where the pilgrims are going to the shrine of Thomas Becket at Canterbury Cathedral.

10   *Universal Living Rosary Association.* St. Philommena, Patroness and Protectress of the Living Rosary. Retrieved from http://www.philomena.org/patroness.asp.

St. Filomena: The young virgin who was martyred at age 13, willingly traded her earthly life for heavenly salvation and continues her work today promoting the virtues of purity and sanctity among the world's youth and bringing the faithful closer to our Blessed Mother and Jesus Christ. It would seem she was held in quiet reserve by God for nearly seventeen centuries and summoned at a time when so much uncertainty and absence of faith abound.

Catholic Online. Saints and Angels: St. Lucy. Retrieved from http://www.catholic.org/saints/saint.php?saint_id=75.

St. Lucy: Lucy's name means "light", with the same root as "lucid" which means "clear, radiant, understandable." Unfortunately for us, Lucy's history does not match her name. Shrouded in the darkness of time, all we really know for certain is that this brave woman who lived in Syracuse lost her life in the persecution of Christians in the early fourth century. Her veneration spread to Rome so that by the sixth century the whole Church recognized her courage in defense of the faith.

11   Tyrell, J. (2012, December 7). Concern over toll on children. *Newsday: The Long Island Newspaper,* 73 (96), p. A 16. "Allison Sarmiento, of Mastic Beach, suggested that the county use social media and other tools to alert residents where disaster recovery centers would be before a storm hits, not after, when chaos reigns. 'Instead of 'Get your flashlights and get your water supplies,' she said 'how about, 'if you're impacted, here are the locations to go to.'"

12   Figueroa, L. (2012, November 5). Voting Sites: Storm damages force some polling places to move. *Newsday: The Island Newspaper,* 73 (64), p. A12. "Nassau has 376 polling sites and Suffolk has 342. It would have taken an act of Congress to change tomorrow's presidential election…To Change the date, Congress would have to override an 1845 law making Election Day the Tuesday after the first Monday in November the 2004 report noted."

13   *CNN 2012 Cable News Network.* Signs of progress, through damage and heartache remain after. 1 November 2012. Retrieved from http://news.blogs.cnn.com/2012/11/01/millions-could-face-cold-weekend-from-sandys-power-outages/

14   Ramos, V. M. & Barrios, J. (2012, November 1). Relief is at Hand: Aid efforts intensify as groups focus on hard-hit LIers. *Newsday: The Long Island Newspaper,* 73 (60), p. A20. "Today, for instance, Long Island

15   Rudd, C. (2012, November 5). Some Relief at Pump. *Newsday: The Long Island Newspaper,* 73 (64), pp. A6-A7.

"Gene Spelman, who owns a Gulf Station in NHP, said since electricity to his business was restored Thursday, he's seen waiting times drop from three hours to 1.5 hours. 'I pumped 8,000 gallons in 10 hours Thursday," Spelman said." The continued with, "The Department of Defense announced Friday it would be distributing more than 250,000 gallons of fuel to NY and NJ through yesterday to assist the Federal Emergency Management Agency's response efforts after Sandy, but gave no specifics."

16 (2012, November 5). Workers raise gas prices by 50 cents a gallon after receiving a new delivery of fuel. *Newsday: The Long Island Newspaper*, 73 (64), p. A14.

17 Laum, C. (2012, December 7). NYC preparing for next big storm. *Newsday: The Long Island Newspaper*, 73 (96), p. A6.

ABOUT THE AUTHOR

Josefa Pace earned a Ph.D. in Literacy Studies, an M.A. in English/Creative Writing, a B.A. in English, and a B.F.A. in Theatre. She has been teaching a wide range of courses for more than ten years at local colleges in New York and California.

Printed in the United States
By Bookmasters